San Diego's Favorite Recipes

from San Diego's Favorite Restaurants

San Diego's Favorite Recipes

from San Diego's Favorite Restaurants

by Joni Halpern
and Christine Calvano

PS Features
San Diego, California

For additional copies of this book, please contact the publisher.
For groups and organizations, a bulk order discount price is available.

Printed in the United States of America

Published by PS Features
P.O. 6751
San Diego, California 92106-6751

ISBN 0-962296-2-1

Library of Congress 91-066687

Cover design and illustrations by Jill Burry and Kathryn Miller

10 9 8 7 6 5 4 3 2 1

To Jeanne Calvano,
who has always cooked with the
most important ingredient of all—love.

Contents

Acknowledgements

It is a formidable task to acquire the permission, information, and recipes of so many restaurateurs and chefs. They are among the busiest professionals you'll find. We thank them all for their time and courtesy and for the care they showed in reviewing our text.

There were many friends who lent us a hand when it was needed. Sofia Armour answered some important questions about technique and ingredients. Harriet Badami gave of her time and knowledge of good food. Janie Mullane shared her enthusiasm and experience as a first-class home chef. Misty Phillips was invaluable in helping construct the glossary. Sam Calvano shared his experience as a first-rate restaurant patron. Young Betsy Drummond was an inspiration in the kitchen.

Some kindnesses must be acknowledged. Chef Tom Horton patiently taught us some fine points only a chef would know. Mary Pappas of Athens Market saved us from collapse on a very long working day. Evelyn Sudora, gourmet cook, showed her skill as a careful editor.

Finally, our thanks to the great restaurateurs and chefs who work so hard to give their patrons something special.

Joni Halpern
Christine Calvano

May, 1992

Introduction

It is the tourist's good fortune to discover that San Diego's wonderful climate and lovely beaches are not the only fine attributes of the city. Along with its natural, historical, and recreational attractions, San Diego offers its visitors some of the finest dining available anywhere. *San Diego's Favorite Recipes* will make it easy for you to choose among the very finest dining places in the city.

Each entry tells a few interesting facts about the restaurant, then lists some of the house specialties you can expect to find on the menu. We include locations, phone numbers, hours of operation, and recommended attire.

But that's not all. This cookbook brings the flavor of San Diego home to your family and friends. The chefs of our city's finest restaurants have shared some of their most treasured recipes, so that you may re-create back home some of the delights of your San Diego visit.

All recipes come from the chefs themselves, so the reader may note some small variations in instructions. We have tried not to tamper with the style of an individual chef, but we have standardized slightly to make things easy for the reader.

A glossary is included so the reader does not have to rely on other resources to understand the various techniques and ingredients used in these recipes. While the list of entries may seem overly inclusive for the experienced home chef, we hope it will encourage others to experiment among the wide array of dishes presented in this book.

Unlike other major cities, San Diego offers fine food at a wide variety of prices. The restaurants included here cover a full range of prices, so there is something for every budget. Since prices change, however, the concerned reader will phone ahead to verify.

Most restaurants today are used to adapting to special dietary needs. If you have such a need, simply call to see what accommodations may be made. You will find most establishments extremely cooperative.

Aesop's Tables

8867 Villa La Jolla Drive
La Jolla, CA 92037
Phone: (619) 455-1535

Just inside the entrance to Aesop's Tables is a world map with near and distant hometowns of patrons marked by colored pins. It's fun to see that guests come from such faraway places as Mongolia or New Zealand. But locals are regular patrons; they seem to regard the food at Aesop's as a periodic necessity.

Aesop's Tables is situated in a typical Southern California shopping center. But the restaurant's interior, with its white walls, photographs, and cozy tables, takes you away to the steep stark towns of Greece huddled on cliffs against a bright blue sea. The restaurant is small and filled with the lively tones of conversation. People come here to enjoy the company of family and friends, but locals also have named Aesop's "Best Place to Dine Alone."

The menu offers a healthful selection of Greek specialties, with a few Middle Eastern dishes to round it out. Ample portions are served. Coffee and desserts are rich and well-loved by the clientele. To enjoy Aesop's food for a picnic in the park or by the sea, patrons may order take-out in person or by phone.

❖ **Hours:** *Monday through Saturday, 11 a.m.-10 p.m.; Sunday, 4 p.m.-10 p.m.*
❖ *Casual attire; no reservations.* **Parking** *in shopping center lot.*
Price: *Inexpensive to moderate. Major credit cards accepted.*

House Specialties

Gyros—a combination of beef and lamb cooked on a rotisserie and sliced thinly; served in a pita bread sandwich or included in a gyros plate

Vegetarian Combination Plate—includes Spanokopita (a spinach and cheese pie wrapped in delicate filo dough) and falafel (a Middle Eastern specialty made from garbanzo and fava beans)

Hummous—a tasty garbanzo bean dip

Tabouleh—bulgur wheat salad with tomatoes, parsley, olive oil, and lemon juice

Soupa Avgolemono

Egg-Lemon Soup

8 cups strained chicken broth (preferably homemade)
1/2 cup rice, uncooked
2/3 cup carrots, sliced 1/4" thick
2/3 cup celery, sliced 1/2" thick
1 large chicken breast, cooked, skinned, boned, and cut in 1/2" pieces
4 eggs, well-beaten
juice of 2 lemons

In stock pot, cover chicken with water and bring to a boil. Add carrots, celery, and rice. Reduce heat and simmer until rice and vegetables are tender. Turn off heat.

Beat lemon juice into well-beaten eggs. Ladle about 1/2 cup hot soup into egg-lemon mixture, mixing constantly. This method prevents eggs from curdling.

Add the egg-lemon mixture into soup pot, stirring continually.

Heat soup very slowly, stirring frequently, until soup thickens. Add chicken pieces. *Soup should never boil.*

Ladle immediately into bowls, topping each bowl with a lemon slice and chopped parsley.

Serves 8-10

Keftedes
Greek Meatball Appetizer

1 lb. extra lean ground beef or lamb (or 1/2 lb. beef and 1/2 lb. lamb)
2 slices good quality bread, soaked in 1/3 cup milk
1/2 cup onion, minced
1/3 cup parsley, finely chopped
1 egg
2 tsp. salt
fresh ground pepper to taste
olive oil

Preheat oven to 375 degrees.

Put meat in a large bowl. Gently squeeze bread to remove milk. Discard milk. Crumble bread into bowl with meat.

Add remaining ingredients, except olive oil. Mix together with your hands until well-combined. Form into 1 1/2" balls. (Dipping your hands into water will keep the meat from sticking to your fingers.)

Lightly brush a baking pan with olive oil. Place meatballs 1" apart on the baking pan. Bake for 20-25 minutes. Let cool for 5 minutes.

Remove from pan with a spatula. Serve with *Egg and Lemon Sauce*, tomato sauce, or by themselves with lemon wedges.

Yields approximately 24 meatballs

Egg and Lemon Sauce

2 cups chicken broth
2 tbsp. cornstarch, dissolved in 1/4 cup water
3 whole eggs, beaten
juice of 1/4 fresh lemon
1 tbsp. butter

Bring broth to a boil. Add cornstarch mixture. Stir and cook over medium heat until slightly thickened.

Beat lemon juice into eggs. Stir a ladle of the hot broth into the egg-lemon mixture.

Stir the egg-lemon mixture into the rest of the broth. *The broth must be stirred as you add the egg-lemon mixture to avoid curdling the egg.* Simmer slowly, stirring constantly, for 5 minutes.

Add butter; stir to melt.

Yields approximately 3 cups sauce

Aesop's Tables' Tabouleh

2 cups raw bulgur wheat, #1 or #2, with scalding water added
    just to cover wheat
1 1/3 cups fresh parsley, finely chopped
2/3 cup onion, finely chopped
1/2 cup fresh mint, finely chopped
1 large tomato, seeded and chopped
2/3 cup fresh lemon juice
2/3 cup extra virgin olive oil
salt and freshly ground pepper to taste
1 large cucumber, seeded and chopped
salt and pepper to taste

Soak the bulgur wheat in the scalding water for 20 minutes. Place in a sieve and rinse under cold water. Drain well. Toss gently with the remaining ingredients. Add salt and pepper to taste.

Tabouleh can be served chilled or at room temperature. Serve in center of large platter, surrounded with chopped cucumber. Eat with pita wedges or roll into lettuce leaves.

Serves 12-16 as hors d'oeuvres

Aesop's Tables' Baklava

6 cups walnuts, finely chopped
2 cups almonds, finely chopped
1/3 cup sugar
1 tbsp. cinnamon
approximately 1 lb. sweet butter, clarified
whole cloves
1 lb. filo dough

Preheat oven to 350 degrees.
Mix first 4 ingredients for filling. Butter one 18" x 20" baking sheet.
Lay one sheet of filo dough on pan, and brush upper side with butter. Continue this procedure for seven more layers of filo dough, laying one on top of the other.
Combine nuts, sugar, and cinnamon. Sprinkle 2 cups nut filling evenly on topmost filo layer, spreading into corners.
Cover this filling with 3 more filo sheets buttered on the top side, then spread with another layer of 2 cups nut filling.
Repeat this procedure two more times. (There will be four layers of nut filling when finished.) Top with 15 to 20 buttered filo sheets.
Cut into 15 squares, and divide those in half diagonally to form triangles. Place a clove in the center of each triangle, leaving the clove standing slightly above the surface. Bake 1 hour at 350 degrees.
Cool to room temperature. Pour hot *Honey Syrup* over baklava and let rest at least 4 hours before serving.

Honey Syrup

3 cups sugar	1/2 cup honey	zest of 1/2 lemon
2 cups water	2 tsp. lemon juice	1/8 tsp. cream of tartar

In a sauce pan, boil all ingredients 20 minutes. Pour hot honey syrup over cool baklava.

Yields enough for 30 servings

Athens Market Taverna

109 W. F Street
San Diego, CA 92101
Phone: (619) 234-1955

It is a blessing for us all that Mary Pappas didn't care for law school. After one year of it, she bought her aunt's tiny, treasured restaurant and market that had served downtown workers for 12 years. Mary's father, who had owned a well-established restaurant in Greece, came over here for six months to teach his daughter the ropes of cooking for restaurant clientele. He left her with time-honored recipes and two rules for success: Never serve your customers something you yourself wouldn't eat, and never let a customer leave unsatisfied.

Mary took those rules to heart, and from them and her devotion came one of downtown's favorite eating places. Athens Market Taverna is a very comfortable restaurant with soft colors, oak bar, white table linens, and sparkling glassware, set off by the aroma of good cooking. Diners linger at window tables over colorful Greek salads, fresh soups, authentic dishes of meat, poultry, and seafood, and a moussaka that has been acclaimed by restaurant critics. The sound of Greek, spoken by Mary and some of her staff, adds to the authenticity of the restaurant.

❖ *Hours: Monday through Thursday, 11:30 a.m.-11 p.m.; Friday &*
Saturday, 11:30 a.m.-Midnight; Sunday, 4 p.m.-11 p.m.
  ❖ *Casual to dressy attire; reservations recommended. Metered parking*
available along streets, free after 6 p.m. and on Sundays. Fee parking available in
nearby lots. Major credit cards accepted. Price: Moderate.

House Specialties

Avgolemono—traditional Greek soup with egg and lemon
Lentil Soup—rich, delicious lentil soup from a secret family recipe
Spanokopita—spinach and Greek cheeses wrapped in light, flaky filo dough
Halibut Sauteed with Lemon and Olive Oil—just like it sounds, fresh
halibut prepared simply and delicately to preserve its natural good
taste and healthfulness

Soupa Avgolemono

1 whole frying chicken, approximately 3 lbs.
2 cups white rice, uncooked
5 eggs
juice of 3 lemons
salt and pepper to taste
4 to 5 quarts of water

Place chicken in a stock pot with 4 quarts of water and salt to taste.
Bring to boil. Reduce heat and simmer for about 1 1/2 to 2 hours. If
necessary, add more water so you will end up with 3 quarts of chicken
stock.

Remove chicken and reserve for later. Strain chicken stock into clean
saucepan and bring to boil.

Add rice to chicken stock and bring to boil again. Reduce heat and
simmer for 30 minutes or until rice is tender, stirring occasionally.

In a large cup, place lemon juice with 1 cup of the chicken stock. Set
this aside.

In a mixing bowl, beat eggs on high speed for 4 minutes. Reduce
speed to medium and continue beating while you slowly pour the lemon
and stock mixture into the bowl.

Into the same bowl, pour 2 cups of chicken stock slowly while continuing to mix on medium speed until contents of bowl are blended well.

Slowly pour mixture from bowl into saucepan of rice and stock,
stirring continuously. Continue to stir for 1 minute while soup cooks over
low heat.

Remove from heat. Add salt and pepper to taste. Serve hot.

You may chop the cooked chicken into small chunks and add it to the soup or use it to make chicken sandwiches or other dishes.

Serves 6-8

Satziki

2 medium cucumbers
3 cloves of garlic
1/2 small white onion
1/2 tsp. white vinegar
1 tsp. fresh dill, finely chopped (or 1/2 tsp. dried dill weed)
12 oz. plain lowfat yogurt

Peel cucumbers. Cut in half lengthwise, and scoop out seeds.

Put cucumbers, onion, and garlic into food processor or blender and mix until smooth. Drain excess liquid.

Pour mixture into bowl. Add vinegar and dill. Mix gently. Add yogurt and blend well. Cover and chill.

Use as dip with bread, pita bread, or raw vegetables.

Yields about 2-2 1/2 cups

Melinzanosalata

Eggplant Salad or Dip

One 1 1/2- to 2-lb. eggplant
3 cloves garlic, finely chopped
4 tbsp. onion, grated
3 tbsp. olive oil
1 tbsp. lemon juice
salt to taste

Preheat oven to 350 degrees.

Pierce eggplant skin in several places with sharp knife or fork. Bake eggplant until very soft, about an hour, then cool. Remove skin.

Chop or mash the eggplant in a bowl. Add garlic, onion, olive oil, lemon juice, and salt. Mix well. Chill before serving.

Serve with bread, pita bread, or as salad.

Serves 8-10 as appetizer, 4-6 as salad

Karodopita
Walnut Cake

1 cup margarine or vegetable oil	4 eggs
1 cup sugar	1 cup milk
1 1/2 cups walnuts, chopped	1/2 tsp. ground cloves
4 tsp. baking powder	1/2 tsp. ground cinnamon
1/2 tsp. baking soda	

Preheat oven to 350 degrees.

Into a large bowl, sift baking powder and baking soda. Add all remaining ingredients. Mix until well-blended.

Grease and flour a 9" x 13" baking pan. Spread mixture into pan and bake at 350 degrees for 30-40 minutes or until it tests done with toothpick.

Cut into pieces and serve with *Honey Syrup* as topping.

Serves 9-12

Honey Syrup

1 cup sugar
1 1/4 cups water
1 half-inch-thick lemon slice
1 cup honey

Combine sugar, water, and lemon slice in a small saucepan. Bring to a boil over medium heat. Reduce heat to simmer for 10 minutes.

Remove from heat and stir in honey. Cool. Remove lemon slice. Pour over walnut cake.

Avanti Ristorante

875 Prospect Street
La Jolla, CA 92037
Phone: (619) 454-4288

Avanti is known for three great pleasures—dining, dancing, and decor. Its menu offers specialties well beyond the breadth of typical Italian restaurants. Franco Ferrandi, born in Milan, Italy, brings to bear his formidable influence as chef and restaurateur in a wide range of authentic Northern Italian dishes. Patrons may dance to live Brazilian music. The decor highlights the smooth, clean lines and nighttime sparkle of modern European design.

Avanti is a place where patrons go to have fun. It's a lively spot. The food, music, and atmosphere are meant to make you feel good, and they succeed, judging by the many patrons who dine there.

❖ *Hours: Tuesday through Saturday, 5:30 p.m.-Midnight; Sunday and Monday, 5:30 p.m.-10 p.m.*

❖ *Dressy attire; reservations recommended.* **Street and fee parking** *available.* **Price:** *Moderate to expensive. Major credit cards accepted.*

House Specialties

Ossobucco—veal shank braised in white wine with fresh vegetables in a tomato base sauce, a specialty of Milan

Risotto with Wild Porcini Mushrooms—rice cooked in broth with white wine and Parmesan cheese, topped with Porcini mushrooms and served with grilled quail

Paella—rice with shrimp, mussels, squid, rabbit, chicken, and pork, seasoned with saffron and peppers

Swordfish Saute

4 swordfish steaks, preferably fresh
1/2 cup olive oil
3 cloves garlic
1/2 lb. fresh fennel
4 stalks celery
3 green onions
1/4 cup white wine
1/4 fresh lemon
1 cup tomatoes, fresh or canned
2 small stems fresh Rosemary, chopped

Rinse fish with water. Finely slice celery, fennel, onions, and garlic. Chop 2 large tomatoes or dice 1 cup canned tomatoes. Remove stem from rosemary and chop.

Heat olive oil. Add swordfish and saute on one side for 2 minutes over medium high heat. Turn fish over. Add celery, fennel, onions and garlic.

Continue to saute for 4 to 5 minutes. Add tomatoes and white wine.

Add rosemary, salt, and pepper. Simmer for 5 minutes. Garnish with lemon wedges.

Serves 4

Chicken Breast Sauteed with Porcini Mushrooms

8 oz. boneless chicken breast
2 oz. butter
1/4 oz. dried Porcini mushrooms
3 green onions, finely chopped
1 fresh leek, finely chopped
2 cloves garlic, finely chopped
1/4 cup white wine
3 tbsp. and 1 tsp. heavy cream
salt and pepper to taste

Remove skin from chicken breast.

Reconstitute Porcini mushrooms in 1/2 cup very warm water. Soak at least 15 minutes. Remove mushrooms and reserve liquid.

In a saute pan, melt butter over medium heat, add chicken, and brown on both sides.

Add chopped onions, leek, and garlic. Reduce to low heat, and cook until completely browned.

Add mushrooms along with wine and reserved mushroom liquid. Over low heat, reduce pan liquids by half, and add cream.

Continue cooking over low heat until desired consistency. Salt and pepper to taste.

Serves 1-2

Ossobucco

6 lbs. veal shank, cut into 6 pieces, each 1" thick
1 cup all-purpose flour
2 tbsp. butter
1/2 cup dry white wine
1 stalk celery, peeled and sliced 1" thick
2 medium-sized carrots, peeled and sliced 1" thick
2 whole garlic cloves
8 oz. can stewed Italian-style tomatoes

Dredge the veal shank pieces in flour, shaking off excess.

Melt butter over medium heat in large skillet. Arrange veal shank pieces side by side in skillet. Add vegetables and garlic.

Brown the veal shank pieces on both sides over medium heat, turning carefully. Pour in wine and continue cooking until wine has evaporated completely.

Add salt and pepper to taste. Add tomatoes. Cover, reduce heat to simmer, and cook meat for about 1 1/2 hours. Add a little water or chicken broth from time to time to keep some liquid in bottom of pan.

Optional: Combine chopped anchovie filets with the grated rind of 1 lemon and 2 tbsp. of chopped fresh parsley. Sprinkle this mixture over top of veal shank pieces before serving.

Serve Ossobucco with risotto

Serves 8-10

Bayou Bar & Grill

329 Market Street
San Diego, CA 92101
Phone: (619) 696-8747

America's constant search for interesting food has made Cajun cuisine popular across the country, especially in California, where you can order a "blackened" version of almost any kind of fish. But the Bayou Bar & Grill is the real thing. Cajun cooking is their specialty and their commitment.

When applied to cuisine, the word, "Cajun" (denoting Louisiana natives of French-Canadian descent), doesn't just mean spicy. There is considerable subtlety involved in creating a taste that is more flavorful than picante. The Bayou Bar & Grill obtains many of its ingredients from the Gulf of Mexico and bayou regions of Louisiana, just to ensure authenticity of taste.

This restaurant has been acclaimed by critics, and San Diegans have proclaimed it best in informal and late night dining. The restaurant's bar offers an intriguing selection of bayou specialties. Bayou Bar & Grill is friendly and comfortable. Decked out in green, white, and dusty pink, the place is just dressy enough, when coupled with the food, that it makes you feel you've been somewhere out of the ordinary.

❖ *Hours: Tuesday through Saturday, 5:30 p.m.-11:30 p.m.; Sunday, 4 p.m.-10:30 p.m.*
❖ *Informal attire; reservations accepted. **Metered parking** free after 6 p.m. and Sundays. Fee parking lots nearby. **Price:** Moderate. Major credit cards accepted.*

House Specialties

Cajun Caviar
Seafood Gumbo
Blackened Fish (the real thing)
Red Beans and Rice with Andouille (a type of sausage)
Cajun Velvet Pie
Creole Pecan Pie

Cajun Caviar

1/2 lb. butter
8 oz. crawfish tails
8 oz. fresh shrimp
1/2 cup celery, chopped
1/2 cup bell peppers, chopped
1/2 cup yellow onion, peeled and chopped
2 tsp. creole seasonings
2 tsp. Lea & Perrin Worcestershire Sauce
2 tsp. dry basil
1 tsp. thyme
1 tsp. fresh garlic, crushed
1 cup green onions, chopped
1 to 2 tbsp. flour
1 tsp. salt
dash Tabasco

Grind to coarse texture in food processor: celery, yellow onions, and bell peppers. Drain and reserve all liquid.

In heavy saucepan, melt 1/2 cup butter, and sautee the above mixture with basil and thyme for about 5 minutes. Remove sauteed mixture and reserve.

In same saucepan, add 1/2 cup butter. Gently cook crawfish and shrimp, adding creole seasoning, green onions, salt, and worcestershire sauce. Cook 5 minutes or until shrimp turns pink. Remove seafood from pan, reserving liquid.

Grind seafood into coarse texture in food processor or blender. Return to saucepan with reserved liquid, and add vegetables.

Add flour, and cook over medium heat about 5 minutes, stirring constantly. Stir in garlic, Tabasco, and salt to taste.

Serve warm and spread over stale or oven-toasted French bread rounds.

Variation: butter bread first with garlic butter.

Use as party appetizer.

Chicken la Combes

2 tbsp. butter
1/2 cup mushrooms, sliced
1/2 cup green onions, chopped
1/2 lb. crawfish tails
1/2 cup water
3/4 cup heavy whipping cream

1/8 plus 1/4 tsp. cayenne pepper
1/2 tsp. salt
1/4 tsp. fresh dill, chopped
1/2 tsp. brandy
4 chicken breasts, 6 oz. each
dash creole seasoning

Sauce:

In medium saucepan, sautee mushrooms and green onions in 2 tbsp. butter. Add crawfish tails and water. Simmer until almost all liquid is evaporated.

Stir in cream, cayenne pepper, salt, dill and brandy. Simmer 5-7 minutes or until mixture thickens.

Chicken:

Sprinkle chicken breasts with creole seasoning. Grill over charcoal until cooked.

Place on serving dish. Ladle crawfish mixture over chicken.

Serves 4

Creole Pecan Pie

9" deep-dish pie shell, pre-cooked
4 eggs
6 1/2 oz. cream cheese
1/4 cup sugar
3 tsp. pure vanilla
1/2 cup light corn syrup
1/4 cup brown sugar
1 cup pecans

Pre-cook pie shell in oven at 400 degrees for 15 minutes. Cool.

Mix cream cheese, 1 egg yolk, 1/4 cup sugar, and 1 1/2 tsp. vanilla. Spread this mixture evenly over bottom of pie shell.

Mix together remaining eggs, brown sugar, 1 1/2 tsp. vanilla, corn syrup, and pecans. Pour mixture into pie shell.

Bake at 350 degrees for about 45 minutes. Let cool, then refrigerate before cutting.

Serve with dollop of whipped cream.

Serves 6-8

Belgian Lion

**2265 Bacon Street
San Diego, CA 92107
Phone: (619) 223-2700**

The terms "packaged," "processed," and "canned" are not in the vocabulary of the Coulon Family. In their long tenure as owners of the Belgian Lion, a favorite among fine restaurants in San Diego, the Coulons have concentrated on the words "fresh" and "made from scratch." Shortcuts that gain time but take away flavor or compromise freshness are just not permitted here. Meals are prepared by Mr. and Mrs. Don Coulon; their daughter is the pastry chef. Other members of the family serve the guests. Dishes are selected for the menu only after they have passed the rigorous review of the entire family—all experts in Belgian cuisine.

The Belgian Lion is known for its excellent preparation of fish, confit of duck, cassoulet, and delicious soups. Both the classical and the Nouvelle French cuisine are reflected in the menu. Desserts are beautifully prepared; the coffee is excellent.

From the lighting to the linens, the Belgian Lion's decor reflects the simple good taste of Europe's old families. Patio dining is available in warm weather.

❖ *Hours: Dinner: Tuesday through Thursday, 5:30 p.m.-10 p.m.; Friday & Saturday., 6 p.m.-10 p.m. Closed Sunday & Monday.*
❖ *Casual to dressy attire. Reservations recommended. **Free parking** in restaurant lot or on street. **Price:** Moderate to expensive. Major credit cards accepted.*

House Specialties

Salmon with Sorrel Sauce—fresh filet of salmon in a sauce of white wine, fish fume, dry vermouth with a reduction of cream, and fresh sorrel

Cassoulet—classic traditional French recipe with lamb, pork, white beans, confit of duck, and herbs

Seabass with Basil—fresh bass sauteed in butter, served with a sauce made from reduction of stock and lemon and finished with fresh sweet butter and basil

Duck Pate

10 oz. ground veal
10 oz. ground pork or pork sausage
10 oz. boned rabbit or boned chicken breast
1 boned breast of duck, 2 if they are small
1 white onion, chopped
salt and pepper to taste
cognac (enough to marinate duck)
2 oz. Port wine

Marinade ingredients:

approximately 1 cup dry white wine
1 white onion, sliced
1 carrot, peeled and sliced
whole black peppercorns
1 branch of fresh thyme
6 whole bay leaves

The day before preparing pate, coarsely chop the rabbit or chicken breast, and let it marinate overnight in white wine marinade. Two hours before baking, slice the duck breast in thin strips, and let it marinate in cognac.

Saute the onion in butter for about 5 minutes. Mix all the meats except the duck meat. Add the onion. Season with salt, pepper, and port wine.

Divide mixture into three portions. Put one-third of the mixture in a terrine (pate mold), then lay half the duck strips on the meat mixture. On top of that, place another layer of meat mixture, then the remaining duck, then the last portion of meat mixture.

Place 6 bay leaves on top of the pate and cover with foil (not heavy-duty).

Place terrine in a pan of hot water, coming almost to the top of the terrine. Bake at 350 degrees until a meat thermometer reaches 140 degrees. (It should take about 1 1/2 hours.) Let cool, then refrigerate at least 24 hours before serving.

Garnish: Usually pate is served with cornichons (little sour pickles) and pickled onions or shallots. But little bunches of grated carrots, red cabbage, and root celery add an extra touch.

Alsacien Onion Tart

4 large onions, chopped
2/3 cup butter
1 tbsp. oil
1 tbsp. flour
4 eggs
1 cup heavy cream
1 cup milk
1 1/2 cups grated Swiss cheese
salt and pepper to taste
dash nutmeg
enough frozen or fresh pie dough to fill 11" quiche pan with high sides

Preheat oven to 350 degrees.
Saute the onions in butter and oil without letting them brown. (It should take about 20 minutes.)
Sprinkle flour on onions. Mix and keep cooking very slowly for

another 10 minutes, mixing continuously, but gently, so onion doesn't turn mushy. Let cool to room temperature.

Beat eggs, cream, milk, salt, pepper, and a dash of nutmeg. Roll out pie dough. Line the quiche pan with the dough. Mix the onion mixture with the egg-and-cream mixture. Pour into dough-lined pan. Sprinkle with a good amount of grated Swiss cheese.

Bake in preheated oven at 350 degrees for about 30 minutes or until brown, making sure that dough is well-cooked.

Serves 6-8

Seabass With Basil

4 6-oz. to 8-oz. fresh seabass filets (1 per serving)
flour
2 tbsp. butter (to cook fish)
3 tbsp. softened butter (for sauce)
1/4 cup chicken stock
1/4 cup fresh basil (leaves only), coarsely chopped
2 tbsp. lemon juice
salt and pepper to taste

Cut the bass into individual portions, removing bones, if any.

Put flour in a plate, turn the bass a few times in the flour, shaking off the excess flour.

In a heavy pan, melt butter. When the butter is hot, but not brown, put in the fish.

Add salt and pepper to taste. Cook fish on both sides for a few minutes. Fish should flake easily, but not be overcooked. Remove fish to a warm serving platter. Discard cooking butter.

Put the chicken stock and lemon juice in the pan used to cook the fish. With a wire whisk, scrape all cooking juices, and over high heat, reduce the stock and lemon juice until syrupy.

Reduce the heat and whisk in the softened butter. Do this over moderate heat, so butter does not melt. This is called "monter au beurre" in French and means "bringing up" or giving your sauce consistency with butter without really melting the butter.

Add basil to the sauce, and cook for 30 seconds or just until wilted. Add salt and pepper to taste. Pour basil sauce on top of fish and serve.

Serves 4

Cassoulet

Ingredients for beans:

1 lb. white beans
1 whole white onion
1 whole carrot, peeled
1 whole stalk celery
1 piece smoked ham or 1 ham hock
1 piece salt pork
fresh thyme
bay leaves
Herbes de Provence
1 head of garlic, finely chopped

Ingredients for meats:

1 to 2 lbs. lamb stew (small cubes)
1 to 2 lbs. lean pork stew (small cubes)
1 lb. garlic sausage (or German- or Polish-style smoked sausage with garlic in it), sliced into 1/2" rounds
1 cup chicken or beef stock
salt and pepper
Herbes de Provence
1 tbsp. tomato paste
1 large white onion, chopped
1 handful fresh parsley, chopped

Cooking the beans:

Wash the beans. They can be soaked overnight. If they are not soaked, they will take longer to cook.

Put beans in a stock pot. Cover with water. Add the salted and smoked pork, herbs, half of the garlic, whole onion, carrot, and celery.

Water should cover ingredients and then some. Cook slowly, checking periodically to make sure there is enough water. The beans will absorb a lot of water, especially toward the end of the cooking period. The beans should be slightly underdone.

Cooking the meats:

In a heavy pot, brown lamb and pork in butter or lard, salt, and pepper.

Add onion, parsley, the other half of the garlic, Herbes de Provence, tomato paste, and stock.

Cover pot, and braise meat slowly. When almost cooked, add sliced sausages.

Putting it all together:

Remove whole onion, carrot, celery, salt pork, and ham from beans. You may cut up the ham and add it to the beans, if you wish. The salt pork is usually too fatty to be useful, and the vegetables should be discarded.

Mix the meats and the beans together, and your cassoulet is finished. The traditional way to serve it is to put it in an ovenproof crock, covering the top with bread crumbs and heating it slowly at a low temperature in the oven until it is nice and hot.

Serves 8-10

Belgian Brown Sugar Pie

enough fresh or frozen pie dough for a 12" pie pan
2 oz. butter, softened
2 oz. light brown sugar
4 oz. creme fraiche (can be found in grocery stores)
2 egg yolks
pinch of cinnamon

Preheat oven to 400 degrees.

Roll out pie dough and line pie pan. Prick dough with a fork. Spread butter on pie dough. Spread brown sugar on dough.

Slightly beat egg yolks with creme fraiche. Pour into pie pan. Sprinkle a little cinnamon.

Bake at 400 degrees for 30 minutes. Let pie cool before serving.

Cafe Budapest

5656 La Jolla Blvd.
La Jolla, CA 92037
Phone: (619) 456-2979

Chef Geza Mayer describes his cuisine as "nothing terribly complicated, just great European cooking." His style, he says, is to prepare fresh ingredients simply, honestly, and in ample amounts. Locals seem to agree with the chef's descriptions, for Cafe Budapest is a favorite for many San Diegans.

The menu brings together some hearty European specialties, including a good variety of Hungarian dishes, as might be expected. Chicken Paprikash, Beef Goulash, Veal Budapest and other delightful foods are typical of the chef's home country. But there are also other interesting dishes from Russia, Germany, and Italy.

American salad and seafood dishes, plus a selection of great sandwiches, round out the menu. Apple strudel, chocolate mousse, and a variety of cheesecakes and crepes comprise a hard-to-resist dessert menu.

Cafe Budapest is located in the Bird Rock area of La Jolla, about three short blocks from one of San Diego's most beautiful sandstone beaches.

❖ *Hours: Monday through Saturday, 11:30 a.m.-9:30 p.m.; Sunday, 4 p.m.-9:30 p.m. Lunch daily, except Sundays.*
❖ *Casual attire; reservations recommended. **Street parking** available. **Price:** Moderate. Major credit cards accepted.*

House Specialties

Chicken Paprikash—sauteed in onion, tomato, paprika, in a creamy
    sauce, served with spaetzle-dumplings
Stuffed Cabbage—Cabbage leaves stuffed with ground beef and rice,
    topped with cabbage gravy and sour cream, served with potatoes
Cucumber Salad—Hungarian style with sour cream
Beef Goulash—Chunks of beef stew in vegetable sauce with paprika,
    served with spaetzle-dumplings

Cottage Cheese Noodles

1/2 cup smoked bacon, cooked and crumbled
3/4 lb. lasagne or wide tagliatelle noodles
1 1/4 cups low-fat cottage cheese
2/3 cup sour cream
1 tsp. lard or vegetable oil
dash salt

    Cut bacon into small pieces. Fry until crispy. Drain and reserve for
later.
    Boil pasta in 7 cups water and 1 tsp. lard or vegetable oil. When pasta
is cooked, drain and turn in bacon drippings.
    Sieve the cottage cheese and pour over pasta. Toss pasta with
crumbled bacon, and pour about one-third of the sour cream over the top.
    Serve on warm plates, with remaining sour cream in separate dish.

Serves 4

Chilled Sour Cherry Soup

(Many other kinds of fruit can be used: black currants, rhubarb,
gooseberries, and apricots are Hungarian favorites.)
1 lb. sour cherries, ripe and pitted
3/4 cup sugar
1/2 lemon peel, grated
1/2 tsp. salt
dash cinnamon
1 tbsp. flour
1/3 cup sour cream

In a large saucepan, heat to a boil 5 cups of water, to which have been
added the sugar, salt, lemon peel, and cinnamon. Boil 3 to 4 minutes.
Taste liquid to see if the flavor is well-blended. If necessary, return to heat
and boil a few more minutes.

Add cherries to boiled liquid and simmer 4 to 5 minutes.

Mix sour cream and flour together until smooth. Slowly stir in one
ladle of hot cherry juice.

Pour sour cream mixture into cherry soup and boil until it thickens.

Cool, refrigerate, and serve chilled.

Serves 6

Budapest Veal Cutlets

8 veal cutlets
3/4 cup butter or margarine
1/2 cup tomato puree
1/4 cup flour
1 1/4 cup mushrooms, chopped
8 slices boiled or cooked ham
8 slices Swiss cheese (mozzarella or jack cheese can substitute)
dash vegeta seasoning (Hungarian seasoning) or meat tenderizer
dash salt

Salt and flour each cutlet.

Heat 1 to 2 tbsp. butter in a skillet, and fry cutlets on both sides till brown. Remove from skillet and reserve pan drippings.

In another pan, saute mushrooms in 1 to 2 tbsp. butter or margarine. Spread mushrooms over cutlets.

Cover each cutlet with a slice of ham and cheese.

Heat reserved drippings. Add tomato puree, flour, 1 tsp. seasoning, 1/3 cup water, and bring to boil for 3 minutes. Spread this sauce in the bottom of a broiler pan or ovenproof dish, and arrange cutlets on top. Brown in the broiler for 5 to 8 minutes or until cheese melts.

Serves 4-6

Lettuce with Warm Dressing

2 heads iceberg lettuce
1/4 cup smoked bacon, cooked and crumbled
1 clove garlic
1/3 cup sour cream
2 tbsp. wine vinegar or juice of 1 lemon
1/2 tsp. sugar
dash salt

Wash and dry lettuce thoroughly, discarding any wilted outer leaves. Cut each lettuce leaf into fourths, place in salad bowl, and sprinkle with sugar and salt.

Fry bacon until crispy, and set aside.

Gently sizzle crushed garlic in bacon drippings. Stir in sour cream and vinegar. Heat almost to a boil. Pour hot dressing over lettuce and toss lightly with crumbled bacon.

Roquefort and Sweet Corn Salad

1 1/4 cups cucumber, sliced
1 bunch radishes, sliced
1 bunch spring or green onions, finely chopped
3/4 lb. firm, ripe tomatoes, cut into eighths
3/4 cup Roquefort cheese
1 1/4 cups sweet corn (fresh, frozen or canned), cooked and drained

In a bowl, mix cucumbers, radishes, onions, and tomatoes. Drain corn thoroughly and add to bowl. Crumble Roquefort cheese over top.
Pour dressing over salad and toss lightly. Serve immediately.

Dressing ingredients:

4 tbsp. salad oil
1 tbsp. tarragon vinegar
dash salt
dash pepper

Blend oil and vinegar together. Add salt and pepper. Mix well.

Serves 4

Cafe Chanticleer

3098 West Point Loma Blvd.
San Diego, CA 92110
Phone: (619) 225-8403

Cafe Chanticleer is a place best described as inventive. Situated in a busy strip shopping center, the restaurant surprises the visitor with a soft interior that seems far away from the cluttered world outside. The menu is extensive and unique. Even dishes that have standard names like "Cobb Salad" or "Swedish Meatballs" have been reinvented to encompass delicious, even surprising new tastes.

Even more astounding are the prices. A substantial lunch, individually prepared, can cost less than a prefabricated meal in a chain coffee shop. The Early Bird Dinner, which consists of soup AND salad, choice of entree and bread, is one of the best buys in town.

It is the high quality of the food that underlines the reasonable prices at Cafe Chanticleer. The quality is ensured by the owner, Chef Eric Pedersen. Pedersen, extensively trained in Europe, has won international acclaim as a chef and has been a successful restaurateur in San Diego for many years. In Cafe Chanticleer, he has created an outstanding menu in a remarkably priced restaurant.

❖ **Hours:** *Brunch: Sunday, 10 a.m.-2 p.m. Lunch: Monday through Friday, 11:30 a.m.-2 p.m. Dinner: 7 days a week, 5 p.m.-10 p.m.*

❖ *Casual to dressy attire; reservations recommended.* **Parking** *available directly outside the restaurant in shopping center lot.* **Price:** *Inexpensive.*

House Specialties

Rack of Lamb—with bread crumbs and Dijon mustard, seared and slow-
roasted

Swedish Meatballs—a tender, delicately spiced version of this Swedish
favorite with a hint of lingonberries

Coq au Vin—traditional French dish of well-seasoned chicken simmered
in wine

Ossobucco—braised veal shank with brunoise vegetables and brown sauce

Brunch Specialties—Swedish pancakes, Elvador Benedict (smoked salmon
Benedict)

Fresh salads—a variety of unique salads featuring such items as chicken,
pasta, and gourmet marinated vegetables, garnished with fruit, in a
delicate honey-mustard vinaigrette

Swedish Meatballs

1 lb. lean ground beef
1/2 lb. ground pork
1 large white onion, finely diced
4 slices white bread
chicken broth (enough to soak bread)
2 eggs
1/8 tsp. ground cloves
salt and pepper to taste

Preheat oven to 350 degrees.

Saute onion until brown. Set aside. Immerse bread slices in chicken
broth. When saturated, remove and squeeze stock from bread.

In a mixing bowl, add bread, onions, pork, beef, eggs, ground cloves,
and salt and pepper to taste. Mix well.

Wet hands. Roll mixture into 3/4" meatballs. Place on sheet pan and
bake at 350 degrees for 10 to 15 minutes. When done, meatballs will have

light coating of whey. Remove by rinsing lightly. Pat dry.

Add 8 meatballs at a time to simmering sauce. Heat through until sauce adheres. Serve with roasted potatoes and vegetables, or serve as appetizers.

Serves 4 as entree

Sauce for Meatballs:

3 oz. brown sauce or canned brown gravy
1 oz. heavy cream
1/4 tsp. lingonberry preserves

In a sauce pan over simmering heat, pour brown sauce or canned brown gravy. Add heavy cream and lingonberries. Stir till well-blended. Add 8 meatballs at a time to heat and cover with sauce.

Coq au Vin

3 whole chickens
1/4 lb. smoked bacon
3 large white onions, medium-diced
5 oz. mushrooms, diced
1 1/2 tsp. thyme
2 bouillon cubes
3 oz. flour
1 1/2 pts. chicken stock
6 oz. burgundy wine
1 oz. Kitchen Bouquet
salt and pepper
dash of soy sauce

Cut chickens in half lengthwise. In skillet, brown chicken on both sides in small amount of oil. Remove chicken and set aside to cool.

Remove breast bones and wings. Separate breast from leg. Cut off knuckle at small end of leg. (The chicken will be semi-boneless.)

In thick-bottomed casserole, fry bacon until brown and crispy. (If casserole dish does not have thick bottom, coq au vin will burn.) Remove bacon and set aside, leaving drippings in casserole.

Saute onions and mushrooms in drippings. Add 1 1/2 tsp. of thyme. As soon as aroma of thyme becomes apparent, add 2 bouillon cubes, stirring until dissolved. Add 3 oz. of flour and stir to thicken bacon drippings. Add 1 1/2 pints of chicken stock. Add burgundy wine.

Stir ingredients well, making sure flour does not adhere to bottom of pot. Add chicken halves. It may be necessary to add more stock in order to cover chicken completely.

Carefully stir to mix ingredients. Bring to a boil. Reduce heat to simmer for about 20 minutes, or until chicken is tender.

Add 1 oz. Kitchen Bouquet for dark, rich color. Add pepper to taste and a dash of soy sauce.

Wine sauce should be napee when finished. Remove chicken. Place on dish. Ladle sauce over chicken. Serve with roasted, gratin, or mashed potatoes and fresh vegetables.

Serves 6

Tart Tatin

Upside Down Apple Tart

8 green Delicious apples, peeled, cored, and cut in half vertically
1 1/2 cups granulated sugar
6 oz. butter, sliced 1/4" thick
1 sheet of puff pastry

Preheat oven to 325 degrees.

Spread 1 1/2 cups granulated sugar in 10" oven-proof saute pan with stainless steel handle. Lay slices of butter on top of sugar.

Over this bed of sugar and butter, place apples, round side down. Heat pan on top of stove over medium heat until sugar and butter start to carmelize (brown). Cook until carmelized mixture is reduced and apples are tender.

Lay sheet of puff pastry, floured and rolled lightly, on top of apples. Place pan in oven and bake at 325 degrees until puff pastry is golden brown.

Protect arms and hands. (Carmelized sugar is very hot and sticky.) Place 11" round pan over puff pastry. Carefully and quickly invert the pan, so the tart drops from the skillet onto the 11" pan. Serve with whipped cream.

Serves 8

Crepe Glace de Framboise

2 eggs
4 oz. flour
6 oz. milk
1/2 oz. oil

Mix eggs well with flour, milk, and oil to make a thin batter.

Heat a little oil in non-stick pan. Pour a small amount of batter into pan, swirling pan to coat bottom. When crepe is golden brown, flip with pallet knife or spatula to brown other side.

Roll 3 oz. hard vanilla ice cream into each crepe. Place on plate. Warm in oven at 300 degrees for about 2 minutes or until ice cream starts to melt slightly.

Pour fruit topping over filled, heated crepes and garnish with fresh fruit.

Topping:

In blender or food processor, puree raspberries or other fresh fruit with sugar.

Casa de Bandini

Bazaar del Mundo
2754 Calhoun Street
San Diego, CA 92110
Phone: (619) 297-8211

Casa de Bandini occupies what once was the home of Juan Bandini, who built it in 1829 on land granted him by the Mexican governor of California. Originally, the house was a one-story structure. While later owners added another floor and some changes to the facade, the thick walls, open-beam ceilings, patio, and many of the artifacts displayed in the interior typify the period of Bandini's ownership.

The Bandini home was the scene of frequent evening balls to which local prominent citizens would come. Bandini himself was a political activist and agitator who welcomed the opportunity to hobnob with those in power. He suffered many financial setbacks, which led to the original sale of his home. It later was acquired by the State of California as an historic site, and remains a legacy of early California hospitality.

Today's restaurant brings color and life back to Casa de Bandini. Works of craftsmanship and art adorn the walls, and waitresses clad in colorful garb enrich the scene. In summer, a mariachi band entertains.

The menu reflects a good selection of traditional Mexican dishes, a certain contemporary California influence of fresh fruits and vegetables, and savory seafood dishes that recall the effect Mexico's vast coastline has had on its cuisine.

House Specialties

Huachinango a la Diana—grilled red snapper with crab legs and
    avocado, topped with spicy jalapeño Bearnaise sauce
Chicken Ysadora—grilled, marinated breast of chicken topped with
    almonds and served with salsa ranchera on the side
Carne Asada and Shrimp—quickly grilled marinated top sirloin and
    butterflied shrimp
Concha de Marisco al Gratin—seasoned crab, shrimp and fish, sauteed in
    butter, brandy, and creamy wine sauce

Black Bean Soup

1 lb. dry black beans
1 onion, diced
1 fresh sweet red pepper, diced
2 fresh California chilis, diced
1 tsp. oregano
2 tsp. salt
1/2 tsp. white or black pepper
5 whole bay leaves

In a non-aluminum stock pot, cover black beans with water and cook for about 45 minutes. Be sure to keep water level at about 2" above beans while cooking.

Saute onion, sweet red pepper, chilis, and spices in 1 oz. vegetable oil.

Pour this mixture over beans while cooking.

Mix the sauteed vegetables and beans gently but thoroughly. Add salt and pepper to taste. Simmer until beans are tender.

Serves 10

Casa de Bandini Fajitas

Marinade:

juice from 2 lemons
1 medium onion, sliced
1 tsp. salt
1 tsp. pepper
1 tsp. fresh garlic, crushed
1 tbsp. Worcestershire sauce
1/2 cup vegetable oil
1 tsp. paprika

Mix together ingredients listed above.

Fajitas:

2 lbs. top sirloin, sliced in 2" strips
4 bell peppers, cut into thin strips
1 large onion, cut into thin strips
2 large tomatoes, cut into thin wedges
1 tbsp. vegetable oil

Marinate sirloin strips in bowl in refrigerator for at least one hour.

Heat 1 tbsp. vegetable oil in skillet on medium high heat. Drop sirloin into hot oil, and saute strips until brown.

Add vegetables, stirring and tossing until tender (4 to 5 minutes).

Serve with hot corn or flour tortillas, refried beans, and guacamole.

Serves 6 to 8

Especial de la Casa

Marinade:

8 oz. beer
juice of 1 fresh lime
1/2 tsp. garlic, minced
2 drops Tabasco Sauce
2 oz. soy sauce
salt to taste

Mix together ingredients listed above.

Meat:

6 portions top sirloin steak, 6 oz. each

Refrigerate and marinate sirloin steaks overnight.
Grill steaks until tender. Serve with hot corn tortillas, guacamole, and salsa.

Serves 6

Crab and Shrimp Fajitas

2 lbs. medium-sized shrimp, peeled and deveined
1 lb. King Crab legs, washed, cracked, shells removed
2 medium onions, diced
5 fresh bell peppers, sliced into 1/4" strips
5 fresh red sweet peppers, sliced into 1/4" strips
1 lb. fresh mushrooms, sliced
3 fresh zucchini, sliced
4 fresh tomatoes, diced
6 oz. soy bean oil
lemon pepper
garlic powder
salt
paprika

Saute all vegetables—except tomatoes—in hot soybean oil. When vegetables are barely cooked, add shrimp, crab legs, and tomatoes.

Season to taste with lemon pepper, garlic powder, salt and paprika.

Stir until shrimp is light pink. Serve with rice, refried beans, guacamole, and tortillas.

Garnishes: (optional)

cilantro
lime slices
romaine lettuce leaves
orange twist
tomato slices
bell pepper rings

Serves 6 to 8

Casa de Pico

2754 Calhoun Street
San Diego, CA 92110
Phone: (619) 296-3267

This is a restaurant for people who want to experience the sights, sounds, and tastes of a Mexican fiesta amid the comfort of a soft California breeze. Casa de Pico is a patio-style restaurant. Locals and tourists alike love to sit under the colorful umbrellas at round, roomy tables, munching on tortilla chips and fresh salsa while they wait for their orders to arrive.

As a concession to spoiled San Diegans, who shiver when the thermometer drops below 72 degrees, outdoor heaters keep the temperature cozy and pleasant. The swirl of color from costumed waitresses and the mariachi band add to the whole experience.

The food is a hit, too. It's fun to try some of the dishes outside the usual Mexican fare. Chili Colorado, steak chunks in a tasty sauce, or the many enchilada variations can really expand your love of Mexican food.

If you approach Casa de Pico at key dining hours, don't be intimidated by the long line snaking alongside the restaurant patio. This line moves fast, and if you get hungry, you can try a homemade corn tortilla shaped on a stone metate, heated, and served with fresh salsa by the "Tortilla Lady."

❖ **Hours:** *Lunch and dinner: Monday through Sunday, 10 a.m.-9 p.m.*
❖ *Casual attire; no reservations accepted.* **Parking** *available in lots or on streets surrounding Bazaar del Mundo.* **Price:** *Inexpensive to moderate. Major credit cards accepted.*

House Specialties

Especial de Juan—refried beans in a corn tortilla shell with carne asada
Avocado Salad—crisp flour tortilla shell with lettuce, chicken, two kinds
    of cheeses, tomatoes, hard-boiled eggs, and avocados
Pollo Fundido—shredded, seasoned chicken with cheese, burrito-style

Albondigas Soup
Meatball Soup

1 lb. ground sirloin, fat trimmed
2 eggs
2 oz. flour
7 oz. rice, uncooked
3 carrots, chopped into large pieces
2 to 3 celery stalks, chopped into large pieces
3 bell peppers, chopped into large pieces
3 large, fresh tomatoes, chopped into large pieces
1 onion, chopped into medium pieces
1 8-oz. can tomato sauce
oregano
garlic
white pepper
salt
cumin

    Boil 1 gallon of water. Add carrots, bell peppers, tomatoes, onion, and tomato sauce to boiling water. Season with oregano, garlic, white pepper, salt, and cumin, to taste. Simmer for a few minutes, and turn off heat, leaving vegetables firm.

Meatballs:

    Mix ground meat with eggs, flour, and rice. Season with oregano, garlic, white pepper, salt, and cumin, to taste. Form mixture into 3/4" meatballs.

Add meatballs to vegetable broth, and cook over medium heat 15 to 20 minutes.

Serves 6-8

Tacos de Carnitas

2 lbs. pork (picnic roast), cut in half
2 oranges, cut in half
2 tsp. garlic powder
2 tsp. white pepper
1 tsp. salt
1 tsp. oregano
1 bay leaf
1/4 cup vegetable oil
3 oz. milk

Put all ingredients, except oranges, in large saucepan. Cover with water. Squeeze oranges over meat; drop orange halves in pan.

Simmer 1 to 2 hours or until meat is tender. Shred meat and serve in hot corn or flour tortilla with: chopped onions, cilantro, and *Salsa Fresca*.

Guacamole and refried beans make this a complete meal.

Makes 12 tacos

Salsa Fresca

Chop:
1 yellow chile (optional)   1/4 bunch cilantro
2 tomatoes   juice of 1/2 lemon
1/2 yellow onion   1/2 tsp. salt
2 green onions

Mix all ingredients and chill.

Makes enough for 12 tacos

Pollo Fundido

1/2 dozen 12" flour tortillas
1/2 lb. mixed grated cheese (jack and cheddar)
2 lbs. shredded Seasoned Chicken*
1 qt. White Cheese Sauce*

Fill each tortilla with approximately 2 oz. of grated cheese and 5 oz. of *Seasoned Chicken*. Fold tortilla burrito-style. (Lay filling in center of tortilla. Fold top and bottom of tortilla one-third of the way over filling. Fold one side over the filling, overlapping with the other.) This should completely enclose chicken filling.

After enclosing filling, deep-fry fundidos (burritos) until golden brown. Place in a baking pan and top with rest of grated cheese and *White Cheese Sauce*.

Bake at 350 degrees for 5 minutes or until cheese has melted. Serve with spanish rice and garnish with sprigs of cilantro.

Serves 6

Seasoned Chicken:

In a stock pot, cover whole frying chicken with water and boil with onion, garlic, salt and pepper, for 45 minutes. Remove chicken, allow to cool, then shred.

White Cheese Sauce:

Combine 3 tbsp. chicken base (bouillon base), 2 cups milk, and 1/4 lb. grated jack cheese in a sauce pan.

Melt together, and bring to boil, stirring constantly. Reduce heat to simmer, and continue stirring until well-blended.

Cafe del Rey Moro

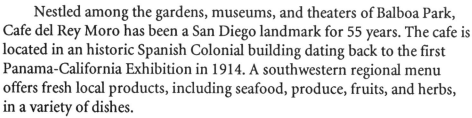

1549 El Prado
Balboa Park
San Diego, CA 92101
Phone: (619) 234-8511

Nestled among the gardens, museums, and theaters of Balboa Park, Cafe del Rey Moro has been a San Diego landmark for 55 years. The cafe is located in an historic Spanish Colonial building dating back to the first Panama-California Exhibition in 1914. A southwestern regional menu offers fresh local products, including seafood, produce, fruits, and herbs, in a variety of dishes.

Sunday brunch at the cafe is a legend. Locals and tourists consider it a highlight of a San Diego Sunday. Guests may sit indoors and enjoy the Spanish-style decor, or they may sit on the lovely terrace looking out over a setting favored for local weddings. For those who are hot, thirsty, and in need of a bite to eat, the cafe offers JC's lounge, serving a variety of drinks, including non-alcoholic alternatives, as well as some tasty appetizer items from the restaurant.

❖ *Hours: Lunch: Monday through Friday, 11 a.m.-4 p.m.; Saturday, 11 a.m.-4:30 p.m. Dinner: Tuesday through Friday, 4:30 p.m.-8:30 p.m.; Saturday, 5 p.m.-8:30 p.m.; Sunday, 4 p.m.-8:30 p.m. Champagne Brunch: Sunday, 10 a.m.-3 p.m.*

❖ *Casual attire; reservations advisable.* **Free parking** *available in Balboa Park lots.* **Price:** *Moderate. Major credit cards accepted.*

House Specialties

Mexican Fiesta (for two)—a heaping platter of carne asada or chicken
asada strips, refried black beans, guacamole, two kinds of grated
cheese, tomatoes, cilantro, lettuce, salsa, sour cream and tortillas

Tortilla Soup—chicken stock simmered with tomato, avocado, tortillas,
onions, cilantro, and jack cheese

Brandy Scallops—succulent scallops simmered in a heretofore secret
brandy sauce with sourdough bread to dip

Margarita Chicken Kabobs—skewers of grilled chicken, marinated and
basted in lime juice and seasonings.

Godfather Pie—a luscious blend of chocolate crumb crust, toasted
almond ice cream, Amaretto, and rich fudge topping

Tortilla Soup

1 corn tortilla
1 1/2 tbsp. grated Monterey jack cheese
1 tbsp. fresh cilantro, chopped
1/2 clove fresh garlic, chopped
1 medium-sized tomato, peeled
2 oz. tomato sauce
2 oz. vegetable shortening
1/4 of an avocado
1 tbsp. fresh oregano, chopped
1 cup chicken broth
1 tbsp. onion, chopped
1/4 tsp. salt

In a blender, combine tomatoes, onions, garlic, and cilantro, and
blend until nearly smooth. Turn into a sauce pan; stir in chicken broth.
Bring to a boil. Simmer for 20 minutes.

Cut tortillas into strips 1/2" wide and 2" long. Fry them in 2 oz. hot
oil until crisp and lightly browned; remove from pan and drain excess oil.

Put tortilla strips in a soup bowl with cheese. Ladle soup into bowl. Garnish with avocado slices.

Serves 1

Brandy Scallops

9 oz. raw scallops
1/2 oz. brandy
3 oz. fresh mushrooms, sliced
1/2 oz. fresh green onions, chopped
2 oz. beef stock
2 oz. whipped butter

In a buttered skillet, saute the scallops until they are cooked halfway through. Add mushrooms, green onions, brandy, and beef stock. Mix thoroughly.

Remove mixture from skillet and place in casserole serving dish that can be heated on stove. Top mixture generously with whipped butter, and bring to high boil just until brown.

Serves 1

Margarita Chicken Kabobs

1 cup lime juice
1/2 tsp. salt
1 clove fresh garlic, pared and minced
2 tbsp. butter, softened
2 tsp. lime juice
1 tbsp. fresh parsley, minced
2 ears fresh corn, cut into 8 pieces
4 tsp. sugar

1 tsp. ground coriander
1 lb. chicken breast, cut into 1" cubes
1/8 tsp. sugar
1 large fresh green or red sweet pepper, cut into 1" chunks

Combine 1 cup lime juice, sugar, salt, coriander, and garlic.

Place chicken in heavy plastic bag. Pour marinade into bag to cover chicken. Marinate in refrigerator for at least 30 minutes.

Blend well: butter, 2 tsp. lime juice, sugar, and parsley. Reserve.

Thread chicken cubes onto skewers, alternating with pieces of corn and pepper. Grill over hot coals, basting with reserved butter mixture for 10 to 15 minutes, turning frequently.

Serves 4

Southwestern Corn Custard

1 tbsp. butter
1/2 cup heavy cream
3 medium-sized whole fresh eggs
4 tbsp. fresh sweet red bell pepper, diced
1 tbsp. fresh cilantro, chopped
salt to taste
5 ears fresh corn
2 medium-sized egg yolks
dash ground cinnamon
1 fresh Serrano chili, seeded and minced
2 tsp. pure maple syrup
freshly ground white pepper to taste

Preheat oven to 375 degrees.

Spread butter over 9" baking dish and set aside.

With a sharp knife, remove kernels and scrape the cobs to extract corn "milk." When mixed together this becomes the corn pulp.

In a mixing bowl, beat together the cream, yolks, whole eggs, cinnamon, peppers, Serrano chili, cilantro, and maple syrup. Add the corn pulp and mix.

Season with salt and pepper and pour mixture into the buttered baking dish. Bake in the center of the oven for 25 minutes.

Serves 12

Creme Brulee with Mangos

10 egg yolks
1/2 oz. vanilla flavoring
brown sugar for topping
1 cup granulated sugar
1 quart heavy cream
1 fresh, ripe mango

Mix egg yolks and sugar in a bowl until creamed. Add heavy cream and vanilla.

In ramekins, put 2 slices of mango and pour in mixture of yolks and cream. Place into pan filled with enough water to go halfway up the ramekins.

Bake 45 minutes at 300 degrees. Cool.

Before serving, apply a thin layer of brown sugar (about 2 tbsp.) on surface of custard and place under broiler until sugar carmelizes.

Serves 7

Cindy Black's

5721 La Jolla Blvd.
San Diego, CA 92037
Phone: (619) 456-6299

Cindy Black is not a tall woman, but hers is a towering presence in San Diego. Her talent as a restaurateur and chef have caused local patrons to name Cindy Black's consistently among their top favorites.

The elegant establishment is a panoply of muted colors and focused lights, against which colorful paintings and lovely table settings make an instant appeal for the guest's eye. The staff are all veterans of fine restaurant service. They never gush over specials; they know their menu, and they always answer concisely if you have a question about preparation or ingredients. Their attention is immediate and courteous, but they appreciate a guest's desire for privacy in this intimate setting.

Cindy Black's offers a menu that caters both to diners seeking a special evening to remember and to those who often dine out. The secret is a menu with a wide variety of selections and prices. Soups, salads, pastas, risottos, and a full range of entrees show an originality that is unsurpassed. The quality of every dish is so consistently good that whether the order is a salad or a full meal, you've gotten your money's worth in uniqueness of taste, freshness of ingredients, and excellence of service.

❖ *Hours: Lunch: Friday only, 11:30 a.m.-2 p.m. Dinner: Tuesday through Saturday, 5:30 p.m-10 p.m.; Sunday, 5 p.m.-8 p.m.*

❖ *Casual to dressy attire; reservations recommended.* **Street parking** *available.* **Price:** *Moderate to expensive. Major credit cards accepted.*

House Specialties

Cassolette of Grilled Sweetbreads—French-style dish of grilled sweetbreads, spinach, and marinated oyster mushrooms, finished with tarragon and madeira
Whole Dover Sole Meuniere
Roast Leg of Lamb with Garlic Mousse and Pan Juices

Pan-roasted Quail with Foie Gras and Armagnac

8 quail, boneless, seasoned with salt, white pepper, sage, and thyme
1 tbsp. clarified butter
8 oz. foie gras, sliced into 8 pieces, seared with salt and pepper
4 tbsp. Armagnac
1/2 cup chicken stock
8 toast points, buttered and halved
1 cup yellow raisins, soaked overnight in 1/2 cup Armagnac and 1/2 cup water

Stuff quail with seared foie gras slices. In a medium-sized creuset pot, saute quail until golden brown.

When quail is golden, cover pan and lower heat. Continue to pan-roast until tender, and leg can be moved easily from thigh.

Remove quail and add 1/2 cup chicken stock. Reduce juices until good flavor develops. Finish by adding 4 tbsp. Armagnac.

Toast buttered bread. Cut into toast points. Keep warm.

Place quail on top of toast points. Ladle sauce from pan and serve immediately.

Serves 4

Turnip Gratin

1/2 cup bacon, uncooked and cubed
6 medium turnips, peeled and finely sliced
3 leeks, cleaned, sliced crosswise, using white portion only
3 cups whipping cream
3 tbsp. Dijon mustard
1 tsp. garlic, crushed
2 tsp. nutmeg
salt and pepper to taste

Preheat oven to 350 degrees.
Saute bacon until almost crisp. Drain.
In ovenproof dish, layer turnips with bacon and leeks.
Combine cream with mustard, garlic, salt, pepper, and nutmeg. Pour cream mixture over turnips and leeks.
Bake at 350 degrees for about 1 to 1 1/2 hours or until turnips are tender.

Serves 6

Crown Room

Hotel del Coronado
1500 Orange Avenue
Coronado, CA 92118
Phone: (619) 435-6611

Few hotels in America have achieved recognition to compare with that of the Hotel del Coronado, made famous in the film classic, "Some Like It Hot," with Marilyn Monroe. A visit to San Diego is incomplete without seeing this beautiful resort hotel built in 1888.

One of the best places to experience the grand scale and fine workmanship of the hotel is in the renowned Crown Room Restaurant with its 30-foot-high domed ceilings.

The Crown Room is known for more than its unique beauty. It is a holiday tradition for many families each Christmas and Easter. Its Sunday Brunch is considered one of the best in the city.

The Crown Room offers a continental menu with tasty preparations of chicken, beef, lamb, pork, rabbit, and duck. Entree salads are inventive presentations of local seafood, chicken, or duck. The service, as expected at the Grande Dame of hotels, is perfect.

❖ *Hours: Brunch: Sunday, 9 a.m.-2 p.m. Breakfast: Monday through Saturday, 7 a.m.-11 p.m. Lunch: Monday through Saturday, 11:30 a.m.-3 p.m. Dinner: Monday through Saturday, 5 p.m.-9:30 p.m. Dinner Buffet: Sunday, 5 p.m.-9 p.m.*

❖ *Casual attire in daytime, dressy at night. Brunch and dinner reservations required. **Valet and lot parking** available in front of hotel. **Price:** Expensive. Major credit cards accepted.*

House Specialties

Grilled Breast of Duck—grilled and served in a honey lime and kumquat
  sauce
Sauteed Saddle of Domestic Rabbit—tender rabbit sauteed, with shallots,
  cognac white wine sauce, and fresh herbs
Rack of Lamb—roasted lamb with a crust of provencale herbs, in a sauce
  of zinfandel and roasted garlic cloves
Del Seafood Salad—shrimp, scallop, lobster, with shallots and fine herbs
  in wine aspic

Cotriade Bretonne

Fish Stew Soup with Sorrel and Leek

bones of white-meat fish for fish stock
10 oz. monkfish filets(without dark meat) or lobster
10 oz. bluefish or sea bass filets
10 oz. red snapper filets
10 oz. flounder filets
4 cups green lip mussels, washed
1 quart fish stock
1 bunch fresh sorrel herbs
4 tbsp. butter
1 lb. potatoes, peeled and cut in 1/2" cubes (Place in water to
  retain color until they are used.)
2 leeks, white part only, sliced thin
2 medium brown onions, peeled and finely chopped
2 cloves garlic, finely chopped
bouquet garni of parsley, bay leaf, thyme, carrot, celery, and
  cracked black pepper
salt to taste
1 cup heavy cream or creme fraiche
6 heart-shaped croutes (pieces of bread, fried till crispy in
  clarified butter, then rubbed with garlic)

To make fish stock, place fish bones in stock pot and cover with at least 2 cups cold water. Bring to boil and simmer no more than 30 minutes.

Wash and dry fish fillets and cut into 2 or 3 pieces. Clean the mussels by washing under running water and scrubbing shell with a brush.

In small pan, cook the sorrel in half the butter over medium heat for 10 minutes, stirring often, until most of liquid is evaporated. Set aside.

In a large sauce pan, cook the onions, leek, and garlic for 2 to 3 minutes in remaining butter until soft but not brown.

Add the fish stock, bouquet garni, salt to taste, and potatoes. Simmer for 5 minutes or until potatoes are slightly cooked.

Add monkfish, red snapper, and blue fish. Simmer for another 3 to 4 minutes, and then add the flounder. Simmer for 3 to 4 more minutes until the fish is nearly tender.

Add the cooked sorrel, the mussels in their shells, and cream. Continue simmering for 2 to 3 minutes, until the mussels open.

Taste for seasoning. Discard the bouquet garni. Serve the stew soup in the cooking pot or in a tureen with croutes in a separate bowl.

Serves 6

Stuffed Capon with Prunes Rennaise Style

10 oz. dried prunes
5-lb. capon (free-range chicken preferred)
5 oz. ground pork, fat and lean mixed
1 shallot, chopped
2 tbsp. fresh parsley, chopped
salt and pepper
1 tbsp. olive oil
1 tbsp. butter
1 carrot, peeled and sliced

1 medium leek (including green top), sliced
1 stalk celery
4 cups white wine (Chardonnay)
trussing needle and string

Soak the prunes in a bowl of hot water for 1 hour (or until softened and plump).

Remove the neck and wingtips from the capon and set aside with the giblets.

Stuffing Preparation:

Drain half of the prunes and chop them.

Chop the chicken liver, and mix well with the chopped prunes, pork, shallots, parsley, and salt and pepper.

Fry a small amount of stuffing until brown, and taste for seasoning.

Capon Preparation:

Preheat oven to 375 degrees.

Stuff the chicken with stuffing mixture, and truss.

On stove top, in a heavy casserole, heat oil and butter, add chicken, and brown on all sides. Add the chicken neck, wingtips, gizzard, carrot, onion, and celery and cook them slowly with the chicken for 2 to 3 minutes, or until slightly softened.

Add the wine, salt, and pepper. Bring to a boil, cover lightly, and transfer to oven, baking for 55 minutes until chicken is tender and a skewer inserted into the stuffing is hot to the touch when withdrawn. If necessary, uncover the casserole towards the end of the cooking time so the chicken browns well.

Sauce:

1 1/2 tbsp. butter
2 tbsp. flour
1 chicken stock or broth
1/2 cup white wine (Chardonnay)

1 egg yolk
1/2 cup heavy cream or creme fraiche

Melt the butter in a sauce pan. Whisk in the flour and cook, whisking constantly until foaming. Gradually whisk in the broth and wine, and bring to a boil.

Drain the remaining prunes, add them to the sauce, and simmer over low heat, stirring occasionally for 30 minutes, or until prunes are soft. Stir carefully to avoid breaking up all the prunes, although a few broken ones will simply add flavor to the sauce. Remove the prunes with a slotted spoon, and set aside.

When chicken is cooked, carve it, arrange the pieces around the sides of a platter, and place stuffing in the center. Keep this warm while finishing the sauce.

Add the sauce to the chicken juices in the casserole, and blend well. Skim off excess fat. Strain the sauce back into the sauce pan, pressing hard on the vegetables to extract their flavor. Reheat the sauce.

Mix the egg yolk and cream in a small bowl, and gradually whisk in some of the hot sauce. Add this mixture to the sauce pan.

Add the prunes, and cook over low heat, stirring occasionally, until the sauce has thickened slightly. Do not let sauce boil, or it will curdle. Taste the sauce for seasoning.

To serve:

Spoon some of the sauce with the prunes over the chicken pieces. Serve remaining sauce separately.

D.Z. Akin's

6930 Alvarado Road
San Diego, CA 92120
Phone: (619) 265-0218

You can afford to be choosy at this deli-restaurant, because there is so much from which to choose. The eight-page menu reads like a Russian novel; by the time you get to the end, you've forgotten the beginning. Every deli-lover's favorite food is sure to be on the menu.

If you're new to the restaurant, the service staff is completely familiar with every item. Portions are ample; even patrons with hearty appetites get more than their money's worth.

On your way out, provided you can still be tempted with thoughts of future meals, you can pick up a few items from D.Z. Akin's huge deli case. Meats, cheeses, fish, salads and prepared foods can be purchased to take home. Fresh baked goods include carrot and cheese cake, strudel, seeded rye bread, bagels, and rum cake, along with many other tempting items.

D.Z. Akins is located just alongside I-8, which makes it a nice place to stop to purchase picnic foods or enjoy a sit-down meal enroute to mountains or beaches.

❖ *Hours: Breakfast, lunch, and dinner: Sunday through Thursday, 7 a.m.-9 p.m., except June through August, when hours are 7 a.m.-10 p.m. Friday and Saturday, 7 a.m.-11 p.m.*
❖ *Casual attire; no reservations.* **Free parking** *in lot adjacent to restaurant.* **Price:** *Inexpensive. Major credit cards accepted.*

House Specialties

East European Favorites—cheese blintzes, lox, borscht, bread pudding, stuffed cabbage rolls, and chopped liver

Deli-style Sandwiches—the awesome triple-decker kind piled high with fine deli meats and cheeses

Desserts—cheesecake (considered by some critics as the best in San Diego), sundaes, shakes, malts, and old-fashioned sodas

Gefilte Fish

3 lbs. pike and carp (or pike and white fish)
1/2 lb. flounder fillets
1 large onion
1 large carrot
1 celery stalk
1 1/2 tsp. freshly ground black pepper
1/2 cup matzo meal
2 eggs, well-beaten

    Preheat oven to 450 degrees.

    Grind fish filets together with onion, carrot, and celery.

    Transfer ground fish to a wooden chopping bowl and chop by hand for a few minutes. Add salt, pepper, matzo meal and eggs, mixing thoroughly.

    Transfer fish mixture to a greased 12" loaf pan, or form into 2 loaves and place in a greased 9" x 13" baking pan. Bake at 450 degrees for 15 minutes, and then lower heat to 325 degrees. Bake 30 minutes longer.

Serves 10

Beef Brisket

5 to 6 lbs. beef brisket
1 lb. canned stewed tomatoes in juice
1 large onion, chopped
2 cloves garlic, crushed
5 carrots, cut into pieces
3 stalks celery, cut into pieces
1 tsp. worcestershire sauce
salt and pepper to taste
1/2 tsp. paprika

Preheat oven to 425 degrees.

In heavy roasting pan on top of stove, bring all ingredients except brisket to a simmer, and cook for 10 minutes. Place brisket in the same pan and transfer to oven.

Roast brisket uncovered for 30 minutes at 425 degrees.

Cover and reduce heat to 325 degrees for 1 hour. Remove cover and continue roasting for 1 more hour at 325 degrees.

Remove brisket and vegetables from pan. Add water to pan juices and bring to a boil on top of stove, stirring briskly. Skim off fat. Add cornstarch, if necessary, to thicken gravy.

Serves 10

Traditional Potato Latkes

5 to 7 medium potatoes
1 medium onion
2 eggs
1/2 cup matzo meal
salt and pepper to taste
vegetable oil

Peel and grate potatoes and onion. Add eggs, matzo meal, salt, and pepper. Mix well.

Drop by large spoonsful into hot, oiled frying pan. Brown on both sides. Pat dry.

Serve hot with applesauce or sour cream.

Serves 6-8

El Chalan Peruvian Restaurant

1050 Garnet Avenue
San Diego, CA 92109
Phone: (619) 459-7707

Looking for a special evening—a bit of romance, magic, and a feeling of being treated like nobility? You can find it at El Chalan. The restaurant is owned by Victor Villar, a trim, handsome Peruvian who offers his guests just the right combination of sophistication and hospitality.

El Chalan's decor is simple, soft, and elegant. Imagine yourself in your own villa, spending a splendid evening with close friends or loved ones. The service is attentive, but not intrusive.

El Chalan has been serving San Diegans for almost 20 years with a fascinating array of California ingredients prepared in the distinctive styles of Peruvian cuisine. Sauces and marinades reflect well-blended flavors of onions, peppers, tomatoes, garlic, cumin, achiote, annatto oil, and cilantro. Mr. Villar serves only the freshest ingredients, perfectly prepared. After all, nobility wouldn't have it any other way.

❖ *Hours: Sunday & Tuesday through Thursday, 5:30 p.m.-10 p.m. Friday & Saturday, 5:30 p.m.-11 p.m. Closed Mondays.*
❖ *Casual to dressy attire; reservations suggested.* **Street parking** *available.* **Price:** *Moderately expensive. Major credit cards accepted.*

House Specialties

Cerviche de Pescado—fresh fish marinated in lime juice and spices, served cold

Anticuchos—beef hearts marinated in spices and wine vinegar, then charbroiled on a skewer

Chupe de Camarones—delectable chowder with shrimp, fish, vegetables, and rice simmered in a seasoned broth

Seco de Cordero—tender lamb stew cooked slowly in a rich cilantro sauce

Pescado El Chalan—fresh fish filets pan-fried and topped with a seasoned sauce of shrimp, scallops, and clams

Cerviche de Pescado

Fish Marinated in Lime Juice and Spices

1 lb. fresh, firm white fish, diced and washed in water
1 medium red onion, sliced thin
3/4 cup lime juice
1 yellow chili pepper, cut in slices
1 bunch cilantro, cut into thin strips, stems removed
2 to 3 tsp. salt
1 tsp. black pepper

Mix the fish, chili pepper, cilantro, onion, salt and pepper. Pour in lime juice and mix well. Let rest for about 20 minutes before serving.

Serves 6 as appetizer

Anticuchos
Beef Hearts Marinated and Charbroiled

1 lb. beef heart, cubed
1 cup wine vinegar
1 tsp. salt
1/2 tsp. pepper
1/4 tsp. cumin
2 tsp. paprika
1 clove garlic, crushed

Mix all the spices and wine vinegar. Pour over the beef heart and let rest 24 hours.

Remove meat, and reserve marinade. Put the beef cubes on a shishkebab and broil or barbecue. Brush on vinegar marinade as beef cooks.

Serves 4

Chupe de Camarones
Seafood Chowder

1 lb. shrimp, peeled and deveined
1 can evaporated milk
1 medium onion
2 whole garlic cloves
1 tomato
1/2 cup green peas
1/2 cup whole kernel corn
1 potato, boiled, peeled, and diced
1 cup rice, cooked
2 eggs, beaten
1/2 lb. white fish filets

Fry fish filets lightly in oil. Remove from pan, dice, and set aside.

Boil shrimp in 6 cups water until pink. Drain, and save broth. Dice shrimp and set aside.

In a sauce pan, saute onions, garlic, and tomatoes in small amount of oil. Add shrimp broth to sauteed mixture.

Boil, add milk, and reduce heat to simmer. Add rice, peas, corn, and potatoes.

Drop beaten eggs slowly into broth, stirring constantly with fork. Do not boil, or eggs will harden.

Dice fried fish and shrimp and add to soup. Heat seafood briefly. Serve immediately.

Serves 4-6

Seco de Cordero

Lamb Stew in a Rich Sauce of Cilantro

3 lbs. boneless lamb
1 medium onion, diced
1 medium tomato
1 small clove garlic, crushed
1/8 tsp. cumin
1/8 tsp. black pepper
1 to 2 tsp. salt
2 bunches cilantro
1 1/2 tsp. paprika
1/8 cup shortening

Brown meat in stew pot. Add onion, tomato, and spices.

Puree the cilantro in blender with 1 cup of water. Pour over meat.

Cover stew. Cook over low heat until meat is tender. Serve with rice.

Serves 6

Pescado el Chalan

Fish Filet Topped With Shrimp, Scallops, and Clams

4 4-oz. fish steaks (halibut, salmon, swordfish, etc.)
8 oz. fresh scallops
8 oz. fresh shrimp
8 oz. fresh clams
1 small yellow onion, minced
1 small clove garlic, crushed
1/2 small tomato
1 tbsp. paprika
salt and pepper

Dredge fish filets in a mixture of flour, salt, and pepper. Set aside.

In a skillet, heat shortening and add onion, garlic, and tomato. Cook over low heat for about 20 to 30 minutes.

Add scallops, clams, and shrimp. Simmer about 6 minutes.

While scallops, clams, and shrimp are cooking, pan-fry the fish filets until brown.

To serve, place one filet on each plate, and pour seafood mixture on top.

Serves 4

Giulio's

809 Thomas Avenue
San Diego, CA 92109
Phone: (619) 483-7726

Giulio's is more than the name of an Italian restaurant. It is a dining adventure begun more than 30 years ago by Giulio Peveri, who dedicated himself to serving the evolving tastes of his patrons. When the restaurant first began, Giulio served pizza, but Americans' exposure to European tastes caused a change in the domestic palate. Giulio responded with a carefully conceived menu of Northern Italian cuisine. This style of preparation is characterized by meats and pasta sauces that tend to be light and delicate, but regular patrons describe the food as exciting.

Ownership and operation of the restaurant remain in the family. Recipes used today are Giulio's variations of classic dishes. Pastas are made fresh, meals are individually prepared, and the elegant desserts are homemade. The menu has become more sophisticated in recent years, but nothing about the food or the atmosphere is pretentious.

Because the restaurant's clientele has increased over time, several dining rooms have been added, each with a different mood. This, coupled with the breadth of menu items, makes you feel as if you've dined in a different place each time you visit Giulio's.

❖ *Hours: Dinner only, Sunday through Thursday, 5 p.m.-9:45 p.m.; Friday & Saturday, 5 p.m.-10:45 p.m.*

❖ *Casual to dressy attire; reservations accepted.* **Valet or street parking.** *Price: Moderate to expensive.*

House Specialties

Scampi Giulio—large prawns with white wine, butter, and fresh
    mushrooms

Tortelloni Verdi—spinach pasta stuffed with ricotta cheese and topped
    with a mushroom sauce

Veal Valdostana—veal cutlets stuffed with prosciutto, cream cheese and
    truffle

Tiramisu

2 cups Mascarpone (Italian cream cheese)
4 eggs, separated
8 tbsp. granulated sugar
42 ladyfingers
2 cups espresso coffee
2/3 cup Cream de Cacao or Grand Marnier
3/4 cup semi-sweet chocolate chips, finely chopped
2 tbsp. cocoa powder, unsweetened

Blend together sugar and egg yolks until the mixture becomes white.
Add Mascarpone.

In a separate bowl, beat egg whites until stiff, and blend into cream
cheese mixture.

Mix espresso and liqueur in another bowl. Dip ladyfingers into
espresso-liqueur mixture, long enough for ladyfingers to absorb liquid, but
not fall apart.

Place 24 ladyfingers in rows on bottom of 9" x 13" tray or glass dish.
Spread half the cream cheese mixture on top of ladyfingers. Make a second
layer of 24 ladyfingers and top with another layer of cream cheese mixture.

Finish by sprinkling with cocoa powder on top. Refrigerate for at least
2 hours, or overnight to thicken.

Serves 15

Veal Valdostana

8 veal cutlets, pounded thin
4 slices prosciutto
4 tbsp. cream cheese
1 small black truffle, sliced very fine
flour
5 tbsp. butter
1/4 cup dry white wine
salt and pepper

Between two slices of veal, place 1 slice of prosciutto, 1 tbsp. cream cheese, and a slice of the truffle. Sprinkle sparingly with salt and pepper.

Seal the edges of the veal by beating edges hard with the dull edge of a knife. Dip lightly in flour, and saute in butter until both sides are golden brown. Add wine, cover, and simmer for 10 to 15 minutes.

Serves 4

Asparagi alla Milanese

1 1/2 lbs. of fresh asparagus
1/2 cup cream
2 tbsp. butter
2 tbsp. freshly grated Parmesan cheese

Cut off tough asparagus ends. Tie asparagus together with string in 1 or 2 bunches.

Pour cold, salted water 2 to 3 inches deep in a tall stock pot. Place asparagus upright in water. Bring water to a boil. Cover and cook over high heat for 8 minutes or to desired firmness.

In a separate pan, combine cream, butter, and cheese over medium heat and bring to a creamy consistency. Lay cooked asparagus on single platter and pour sauce over top.

Serves 4-6

Zabaglione Caldo con Fragole

1 to 2 baskets fresh strawberries, washed and stems removed
4 egg yolks
4 tbsp. sugar
1/2 cup sweet marsala wine
pinch of cinnamon

In the top half of a double boiler, place egg yolks and sugar. Heat and stir these ingredients until the mixture acquires a smooth consistency.

At this point, add the 1/2 cup marsala wine, pouring in a little at a time, while continuing to stir vigorously. Add pinch of cinnamon.

Whisk into pale golden froth, and pour over strawberries.

Serve in clear glass goblets.

Serves 4

Torte de Sandra

Crust:

9" springform pan (bottom and sides thoroughly buttered)
5 tbsp. unsalted butter, melted
1 cup chocolate wafer cookies, finely ground
1 cup toasted almonds, finely ground
2 tbsp. granulated sugar

Combine all ingredients. Mix well. Press mixture into bottom of buttered springform pan and refrigerate.

Torte:

6 eggs
1 tsp. vanilla
1/3 cup flour
1/4 cup granulated sugar
16 oz. semi-sweet chocolate squares or chocolate chips
1 cup fresh whipping cream

Preheat oven to 325 degrees.

In a mixing bowl, beat 6 eggs and 1 tsp. vanilla at low speed with electric mixer. Add flour and sugar. Beat at high speed for about 10 minutes. Set aside.

Melt semi-sweet chocolate and 1/2 cup whipping cream. Blend together. Add 1/4 of egg mixture into chocolate. Mix well. Add the remaining egg mixture into chocolate and blend. Beat the remaining 1/2 cup whipping cream until soft peaks form. Fold into chocolate mixture.

Pour mixture into refrigerated crust and bake at 325 degrees for 30 to 35 minutes. Cool 3 to 4 hours. Release springform pan. Place torte on serving cake platter. Serve at room temperature or chilled, with piped borders of Chocolate Whipped Cream Topping.

Chocolate Whipped Cream Topping:

2 cups whipping cream
2 tbsp. powdered cocoa, unsweetened
3 tbsp. confectioner's sugar

Beat whipping cream until stiff peaks form. Add cocoa and confectioner's sugar. Put into pastry bag and pipe a border on the bottom and top of torte.

Serves 10

Prosciutto e Melone

2 sweet medium-sized cantaloupes
12 slices top-quality imported prosciutto (sliced very thin)

Cut each cantaloupe into six slices. Remove the rind. Wrap one slice of prosciutto around each cantaloupe slice. Place on a large platter and serve at room temperature.

Serves 6-8

Pasatelli in Brodo

10 cups meat broth
3/4 cup freshly grated Parmesan cheese
1/2 cup dry, unflavored bread crumbs
1/4 tsp. grated nutmeg
2 large eggs
extra Parmesan cheese

On a pastry board, combine the 3/4 cup Parmesan cheese with bread crumbs and nutmeg. Mix very well. Add the eggs, and mix thoroughly. Work into a ball. The dough must be smooth and moldable.

Bring broth to a boil in a large saucepan. Put the dough into a ricer, and rice directly into broth. Reduce heat, and simmer for 1 to 2 minutes. Serve piping hot with fresh Parmesan cheese.

Serves 4-6

Hamburguesa!

**Bazaar del Mundo
4016 Wallace Street
San Diego, CA 92110
Phone: (619) 295-0584**

At Hamburguesa!, the combination of patterns played out in stained glass, tile, and fabric capture the eye. The antiques of old California incite the imagination. It is possible in this artistic and decorative environment to forget why you came here. Undoubtedly, your purpose is to sample some tasty Mexican and California variations on the favorite American food, the hamburger. Hamburguesa! also takes pride in presenting some low-calorie, low cholesterol, but tasty, variations on typical Mexican dishes, in addition to offering popular preparations.

Hamburguesa!, part of Bazaar del Mundo, looks out on a small park in Old Town where festivities celebrating Cinco de Mayo and other occasions take place. Marimba players perform at the restaurant on weekends. Patio dining is available. On your way out, you can pick up a souvenir map of Old Town designed by Bazaar del Mundo's artist, Dierdre Lee.

❖ **Hours:** *Monday through Saturday, 11 a.m.-10 p.m.; Sunday, 10 a.m.-10 p.m. Brunch: Sunday, 10 a.m.-Noon.*
❖ *Casual attire; Reservations accepted.* **Free parking** *along street or in lots surrounding Bazaar del Mundo.* **Price:** *Inexpensive to moderate. Major credit cards accepted.*

House Specialties

Pollo Blanco—boneless chicken breast served over rice with whole green
    chilis, jack cheese, and a special sauce
Chili Pablano—chilis stuffed with chicken and cheese and covered
with verde sauce (made from tomatillos)
Gourmet Hamburgers—tasty variations on the beloved burger

Healthy Enchiladas

1 dozen corn tortillas
1 cup jack cheese, grated
1 large can Ortega chilis, chopped
1 small can black olives, pitted and sliced
3 cups *Verde (tomatillo) Sauce*

Cover bottom of a 9" x 13" pan with *Verde Sauce*. Individually dip
tortillas on each side in Verde Sauce.

Lay tortillas on bottom of pan, and fill each with 2 oz. *Seasoned
Chicken* and 2 tbsp. Ortega chiles. Roll into enchiladas by folding one side
of tortilla over filling and overlapping the other side to close.

Pour remaining verde sauce (about 2 cups) over enchiladas.

Sprinkle each enchilada with 1 oz. jack cheese. Bake at 350 degrees
for approximately 20 minutes.

Sprinkle enchiladas with black olives. Serve with shredded lettuce,
chopped tomatoes, and green onions.

(NOTE: For even healthier enchiladas, omit the jack cheese; bake and
sprinkle with Parmesan cheese.)

Serves 4-6

Verde (Tomatillo) Sauce

4 lbs. fresh tomatillos, dry outer skin removed
7 yellow chilis (number can vary, depending on spiciness desired)
1 onion, chopped or in small chunks
1 small bunch cilantro
1/2 tsp. salt
1/2 tsp. sugar
1 tsp. garlic
1/2 to 1 cup water

Boil tomatillos about 15 to 20 minutes. Drain. Cool with cold water. In blender, blend all ingredients until smooth.

Yield: 1 quart

Chili Poblano

Seasoned Chicken

8 fresh California chilis or canned Ortega Chilis
16 oz. grated jack/cheddar cheese
2 cups **Verde Sauce***

Blanch chilis in boiling water. Peel off outer skin. Let cool.
Slit chilis open lengthwise. Stuff each with about 5 oz. of chicken and 2 oz. cheese.
Lay chilis in 9"x13" pan. Cover with Verde Sauce. Sprinkle with grated cheese. Heat in oven at 350 degrees for 20 minutes. Serve with rice and beans if desired.

Serves 4

Seasoned Chicken

1 whole frying chicken
1 onion, quartered
2 cloves garlic, peeled and halved
salt and pepper

Cover chicken with water in stock pot. Add onion, garlic, salt, and pepper. Boil for 45 minutes.

Let chicken cool and shred meat from bone.

Vegetarian Tacos

2 oz. refried beans
2 oz. gaucamole (mashed, seasoned avocado)
2 oz. lettuce, shredded
1 oz. alfalfa sprouts
1 oz. *Salsa Mesa*
2 oz. jack/cheddar cheese, grated
1 oz. tomatoes, chopped
1 tbsp. sunflower seeds
2 warm 10" flour tortillas

Inside each tortilla, layer all ingredients as listed above. Serve with Mexican rice.

(Note: Beans can be canned or made fresh using pinto beans, 3 cloves garlic, 1 large chopped onion, salt and pepper. Cook according to package directions until tender. Drain and mash as you would potatoes.)

Serves 1-2

Salsa Mesa

3 to 6 yellow chilis, chopped (Number depends on desired spiciness.)
3 lbs. tomatoes, chopped
1 large onion, chopped
1 bunch cilantro, chopped
1/2 bunch green onions, chopped
2 tbsp. crushed red chilis
2 tsp. garlic powder
1 tsp. black pepper
2 tsp. salt
1 12- to 16-oz. can tomato sauce, plus 1 can water

Combine all ingredients. Mix well and serve.

Yields about 1 quart

Harbor House

Seaport Village
831 West Harbor Drive
San Diego, CA 92101
Phone: (619) 232-1141

Harbor House is a perfect vacation restaurant. Even the locals feel as if they've been on vacation after eating there. The setting is perfect—in the heart of Seaport Village looking across the harbor at the Coronado Bridge and Coronado Island. Naturally, the house specialty is fish, and it has to be among the freshest fish served in the entire city. Everyday, fisherman offload their catch along this very waterfront, and Harbor House chefs take their pick.

Patrons may dine indoors or on the deck. In either case, the view is magnificent, and the service is excellent. Before or after dinner, it's fun to browse through the shops of Seaport Village or join the small parade of humanity that strolls along the boardwalk.

❖ *Hours: Brunch: Sunday, 10 a.m.-2:30 p.m. Lunch: Monday through Saturday, 11:30 a.m.-3 p.m. Dinner: Monday through Thursday, 5 p.m.-10 p.m.; Friday, 5 p.m.-11 p.m.; Saturday, 4:30 p.m.-11 p.m., and Sunday, 4:30 p.m.-10 p.m.*

❖ *Casual attire; reservations recommended.* **Free parking** *for limited time in Seaport Village parking lots; parking rates apply afterward.* **Price:** *Moderate to expensive. Major credit cards accepted.*

House Specialties

Absolutely Fresh Fish—as many as 18 varieties of fish delivered right from the boats, served broiled, smoked, blackened, or with special sauces

Cioppino—the traditional San Francisco Italian fisherman stew—fresh fish simmered in a broth of tomatoes, wine, olive oil, and seasoning, with shrimp, crab, scallops, and clams added

Salmon in Pastry—delicate filets of fresh salmon in a light pastry with Jarlsberg and Romano cheeses, served in a cream sauce of fresh basil, mushrooms, and cognac

Charred Rare Ahi

Marinade:

5 tbsp. Indonesian soy sauce (Balikat Jap)
3 tbsp. regular soy sauce
3 tbsp. sesame oil
1 tsp. garlic, minced
1/2 tsp. fresh ginger, minced

Whisk all ingredients together and re-whip before each use. Reserve separately 2 tbsp. plus 1 1/2 tsp. marinade to be used in salad dressing.

Ahi (Yellowfin Tuna):

8 oz. strip of top quality fresh ahi, cut into 1" x 1 1/2" slices

Rub fish slices with some of the marinade. Put in freezer until the outer 1/16" is frozen. This is done to keep the fish raw when the outside is seared.

Fish can be seared up to 4 hours in advance. In a red-hot cast iron skillet, put a light char on the outside of the tuna, without cooking more than 1/8" deep from the outer surface. After the fish is seared, rub it with more of the marinade. Cover and refrigerate.

When ready for use, slice the fish as thinly as possible, and arrange on the front of 4 plates. Very lightly, brush the slices with some marinade before putting on plate.

Greens:

various kinds of lettuce, which may include raddichio, lambs lettuce (manche), and others
*Dressing
   Lightly toss greens with dressing. Arrange on back of each plate, keeping ahi at the front.

*Dressing:

6 tbsp. extra virgin olive oil
2 tbsp. plus 1 1/2 tsp. of marinade (above)
1 tbsp. plus 1 1/2 tsp. Balsamic vinegar
   Mix together all ingredients.

Avocado:

Use 1/4 avocado for each plate. Slice avocado on the bias and fan the slices on the plate. Sprinkle the light-colored part of the avocado with black sesame seeds and the green part with white sesame seeds.

Crab Imperial

1 2-lb. blue crab, cracked, meat removed, shell reserved
2 eggs
1/2 cup mayonaise
1 1/2 tsp. Worcestershire sauce
1/2 tsp. salt
1/8 tsp. thyme
1/8 tsp. dried oregano
1/8 tsp. dry mustard

Preheat oven to 350 degrees.

Wash crab shell. Place in covered pot and boil with 1 tsp. baking soda for 20 minutes. Drain, rinse, and pat dry.

Combine crab meat and remaining ingredients. Stuff mixture into body of blue crab shell. Place in ovenproof dish and bake at 350 degrees for 12 minutes. Serve immediately.

Variation: Bread crumbs may be sprinkled on top. Brown in oven.

Serves 10 (4-oz. servings)

Islandia Bar and Grill

Hyatt Islandia Hotel
1441 Quivira Road
San Diego, CA 92109
Phone: (619) 224-1234

Sometimes vacationers shy away from typical hotel dining rooms, anticipating sterile decor and undistinguished food. But the visitor to Islandia Bar and Grill, part of the beautiful Hyatt Islandia Hotel, will be delightfully surprised, for this restaurant brings together good food and a sample of San Diego's paradise surroundings.

The focus of the restaurant's design is the bay view that wraps the dining room in clear skies, calm waters, and colorful sailboats. Chairs are comfortable, tables spacious, and the room is bright with natural light in daytime. At night, running lights wink from boats on the bay.

The menu offers several well-prepared dishes featuring chicken, beef, vegetables and fruit, including a fixed-price buffet with a stunning array of coldcuts, vegetable salads, fruits, meats, side dishes and desserts. For the guest seeking a unique cuisine, the restaurant offers, among other items, wholesome, fresh Italian specialties and seafood.

Favorites among meal starters are cioppino and a unique antipasto salad with marinated clams, mushrooms, and squid, along with roasted peppers, cheeses, and Italian coldcuts. Pasta dishes have a light, carefully seasoned tomato sauce, and the pasta itself is never overcooked. Seafood dishes, whether grilled or fried, are freshly prepared. Desserts are as sinful as they should be for someone on vacation, and the service is prompt, informed, and friendly.

❖ **Hours:** *Brunch: Sunday, 9:30 a.m.-2 p.m. Lunch: Monday through Saturday, 11 a.m.-5 p.m.; Sunday, Noon to 5 p.m. Dinner: Monday through Saturday, 6 p.m.-10:30 p.m..*

❖ *Casual attire for lunch and brunch, casual to dressy attire for dinner. Reservations recommended.* **Parking** *along street or in lots adjacent to hotel complex.* **Price:** *Moderate to expensive. Major credit cards accepted.*

House Specialties

Grilled Ahi—loin of tuna with ragout of red onions, fennel, mushrooms, and vermouth

Mixed Seafood Grill—grilled shrimp, fresh scallops, and swordfish basted in herbs and olive oil

Penne Arrabbiata—penne noodles cooked al dente and served in a spicy tomato sauce with basil, garlic, and crushed red chili peppers

Whole Fried Fish with Sesame Cucumbers and Tomato Salad

Fish:

2 lb. whole red snapper (or any type of whole fish, such as striped bass, catfish, etc.)

6 oz. flour

6 oz. cornstarch

2 oz. soy sauce

sunflower greens or alfalfa sprouts

Mix flour and cornstarch together. Baste whole fish with 2 oz. soy sauce. Roll fish in flour and cornstarch mixture.

In fryer or in large metal pot, heat oil (enough to submerge fish) to 350 degrees (about medium high heat). Place fish in oil and fry 7 to 10 minutes or until golden brown.

If fish is not quite done in that amount of time, finish cooking in oven at 350 degrees. Remove from oven.

Ladle *sauce* over fish. Top with sunflower greens or alfalfa sprouts.

Sauce:

6 oz. soy sauce
2 oz. sesame oil
1 small red or white onion, sliced
2 bunches green onions, chopped
2 oz. fresh ginger, grated

In large bowl, mix together soy sauce, sesame oil, red or white onions, green onions, and grated ginger.

Sesame Cucumber Salad:

1 medium cucumber
1 medium tomato
2 oz. sesame oil
pinch of crushed red chili pepper

Wash and slice cucumber. Cut tomato into eighths. Toss cucumber and tomato with sesame oil and crushed red chili pepper. Serve cucumber salad as accompaniment on same platter, near tail of fish.

Serves 2-4

Mixed Seafood Grill

3 oz. swordfish steak
3 shrimp, peeled and deveined
3 scallops
1 lemon, cut in half
salt and pepper to taste
3 oz. olive oil
fresh basil, thyme, and chives, chopped

Mix basil, thyme, and chives with 3 oz. olive oil and juice of half a lemon. Prior to grilling, use mixture to oil all pieces of seafood. Also use this mixture for basting the seafood while grilling.

Place swordfish on grill. One minute later, place shrimp on grill.

A minute later, place scallops on grill. Cook for about 2 minutes more, then turn, basting with oil mixture. Grill for an additional 2 to 3 minutes.

Remove seafood from grill. Place on warm platter. Baste again with oil mixture. Serve with lemon.

Seafood may be served with rice pilaf, butter noodles, roasted potatoes and fresh vegetables.

Penne Arrabbiata

10 oz. penne noodles
2 medium vine-ripened tomatoes, chopped
1 small bunch fresh basil leaves
pinch of crushed red chili peppers
3 cloves fresh garlic, minced
1 tsp. Parmesan cheese
10 Calamata olives, pitted and chopped
3 tsp. olive oil
salt to taste

Cook penne noodles in boiling water with a pinch of salt and 1 tsp. olive oil. When pasta is just tender, drain and set aside.

Saute olives, red chili peppers, tomatoes, and garlic for 3 minutes. Then let simmer for 2 minutes.

Add fresh basil and noodles to sauce. Toss until noodles are well covered. Season to taste. Place pasta in warm serving dish. Top with Parmesan cheese.

Serve with warm garlic bread and fresh vegetables.

Serves 2-3

La Gran Tapa

611 B Street
San Diego, CA 92101
Phone: (619) 234-8272

Something about this Spanish restaurant stays with you. It's not just the food, which is colorful, delicious, and inspiring. It's not just the romantic and charming atmosphere, which recalls in a warm-hearted way the Spanish homeland. It's a feeling that hospitality is prized here, and everything is like a gift. From the host's greeting at the door, through a delightful excursion into authentic Spanish cuisine, to the hum of happy conversation around you, La Gran Tapa makes you feel at home.

The menu spans an awesome range, with plenty of unusual choices among standard categories of appetizers, salads, soups, side dishes, entrees, and desserts. La Gran Tapa takes pride in the authenticity, presentation, and fine taste of its cuisine. Whether it's steak or chicken livers, appetizer or entree, the chef takes everything seriously here. It makes people want to come back to try the rest of the menu. It's a big job, but a growing number of regular customers are trying to do it.

Situated among the banks and law firms of downtown, La Gran Tapa is a welcome respite from a busy city.

❖ *Hours: Brunch: Sunday, 11 a.m.-3 p.m. Daily: Monday, 11:30 a.m.-10 p.m.; Tuesday through Thursday, 11:30 a.m.-11 p.m.; Friday & Saturday, 11:30 a.m.-Midnight. Sunday: Dinner, 4 p.m.-9 p.m.*

❖ *Casual to dressy attire; reservations required.* **Metered street parking** *and fee parking available. Street parking free after 6 p.m. and on Sundays.* **Price:** *Moderate to expensive. Major credit cards accepted.*

House Specialties

Paella—traditional Spanish dish made with rice, seafood, chicken, and pork, seasoned with saffron

Zarzuela—saffron-seasoned stew with fish, shrimp, crab, scallops, and clams

Faba Asguriana—stew made with white beans, an assortment of Spanish sausages, pork, and paprika

Black Bean Soup

1 cup bell pepper, chopped
1 cup brown onion, chopped
1/2 bunch celery, chopped
2 smoked ham hocks
2 tbsp. beef bouillon, dissolved in hot water
5 bay leaves
2 tsp. oregano
1 tbsp. salt
1 tbsp. pepper
1 tsp. crushed red chili pepper
1 tbsp. cumin
1/4 cup red wine vinegar
1 tsp. rosemary
5 lbs. dry black beans, soaked overnight and drained

In a stock pot, brown ham hocks in 1 to 2 tbsp. oil. Add vegetables and sweat.

Fill pot with water to 2" above beans. Add beef bouillon, herbs, and seasonings and simmer for 6 to 8 hours.

Add water from time to time to keep beans loose. Near end of cooking time, add red wine vinegar.

Serves 15-20

Chicken Livers in Cream-Sherry Sauce

10 chicken livers
1 to 2 tbsp. olive oil
1/2 tsp. fresh garlic, minced
5 oz. cream
2 oz. butter
1/2 tsp. fresh parsley, chopped (or dry parsley)
1 oz. brandy
2 oz. dry white wine
2 oz. cooking sherry
1/4 cup chopped white onions
1/2 cup sliced fresh mushrooms

Sprinkle livers with salt, pepper, and flour. In a skillet over high heat, brown livers in 1 to 2 tbsp. olive oil.

Add garlic, onions, and mushrooms. Flame all ingredients with brandy.

Add white wine, butter, and sherry. Reduce heat to medium, and add cream. Cook for 5 to 10 minutes until done. Sprinkle with parsley and serve.

Serves 2

Lamb Brochettes

1 leg of lamb, cut into 1 1/2" cubes
2 red onions, cut into 1" slices

Marinade:

1/4 tsp. Spanish paprika
1/2 tsp. crushed red chili pepper
1/2 tsp. Greek oregano
1/2 tsp. cumin
3/4 tsp. Kosher salt
1/4 cup fresh garlic, minced
1/4 tsp. ground black pepper
1/2 cup olive oil

Mix all marinade ingredients thoroughly. Place lamb in marinade and refrigerate for 24 hours.

Remove lamb from marinade. Thread alternating pieces of lamb and red onion on skewer. Grill.

Serves 4-6

L'Auberge

1237 Prospect Street, Suite P
La Jolla, CA 92037
Phone: (619) 454-2524

Tucked away just a few steps off the Prospect Street promenade, L'Auberge is a welcome touch of the Old World in the midst of the new. The restaurant is small, romantic, and sophisticated. Owners Andre and Danielle Lemaire, originally from France, have been serving San Diegans for more than 25 years. Their goal has been to provide the best of traditional French cuisine. Chef Frederic Pierrel takes pride in serving lovely and delectable presentations of California's produce, meats, and fresh seafood. Thankfully, his desserts are traditional as well; they are rich, but not heavy, and they are artfully done.

The Lemaires want to give their guests a meal as authentically French as one that might be served on the French Riviera. Certainly, the location supports that effort, and critics and patrons alike highly acclaim the food.

❖ *Hours: Lunch: Monday through Saturday, 11:30 a.m.-2 p.m. Dinner: Monday through Saturday, 6 p.m.-10 p.m.*
❖ *Casual to dressy attire; dinner reservations required Friday and Saturday.* **Free and metered street parking,** *as well as fee parking available in daytime. Free street parking and fee parking available at night.* **Price:** *Expensive. Major credit cards accepted.*

House Specialties

Halibut au Fenouil—poached halibut on a fennel seed sauce
Sole Meuniere—sauteed fresh Dover sole with butter, lemon juice, and
    parsley
Stuffed Chicken Breast—fresh breast of chicken stuffed with veal, onions,
    shallots, and fresh basil, served with an orange sauce

Fresh Sea Bass and Fresh Fennel

4 8-oz. fresh sea bass filets (1 per serving)
2 heads of fresh fennel
1 cup heavy cream
1 tbsp. butter
1 tbsp. olive oil

Wash fennel in cold water, and slice into fine pieces. Saute fennel in a
pan with butter.

While the fennel is cooking, season fish on a plate with olive oil, salt,
and pepper.

When fennel is cooked soft and tender, add the cream, and reduce
until thick. Salt to taste. Keep sauce warm.

Saute or grill the fish. Spread the sauce on individual plates, and place
cooked fish on top.

Can be served with fresh pasta.

Serves 4

Sauteed New York Steak with Cabernet Sauvignon and Shallot Sauce

4 New York steaks
2 large shallots, sliced
6 oz. Cabernet Sauvignon wine
2 tbsp. butter
salt and pepper
1 tbsp. fresh parsley, chopped
1 tbsp. brown gravy

Saute steaks until cooked as desired (medium-rare suggested). Set aside.

In the same pan, add shallots and butter. Let the shallots sweat slowly (1 minute).

Turn heat to high. Add wine and reduce by one-fourth.

Add the gravy and boil sauce again. Stir with wire whip, and add 1 additional tbsp. of butter to smooth sauce. Whip quickly.

Add salt and pepper as desired. Add chopped parsley.

Put sauce on top of each steak. Serve with potatoes.

Serves 4

Lino's

Bazaar del Mundo
2754 Calhoun Street
San Diego, CA 92110
Phone: (619) 299-7124

Lino's Italian Restaurant has thrived in the heart of Old Town—the symbol of San Diego's Mexican heritage. But don't look for red chianti bottles or checkered tablecloths, for this establishment shares in the great whirl of color and atmosphere that characterizes all of Bazaar del Mundo in Old Town. Lino's is a cozy place with intimate booths, red tablecloths, cane chairs, tile floors, and walls decorated in colorful collage or fabric.

Lino's offers traditional red-sauce Italian dishes, but it also serves meats, pasta, and shrimp with a variety of other sauces. The menu offers a nice selection of salads with fresh fruits and vegetables typical of Southern California. Patio dining on weekends.

❖ *Hours: Lunch: Monday through Sunday, 11 a.m.-4 p.m. Dinner: Sunday through Thursday, 5 p.m.-9 p.m.; Friday & Saturday, 5 p.m.-9:30 p.m. Limited menu served between 4 p.m. and 5 p.m. everyday.*
❖ *Casual attire; reservations required. **Parking** available on streets or in lots surrounding Bazaar del Mundo. **Price:** Inexpensive to moderate. Major credit cards accepted.*

House Specialties

Scampi Italiano—large butterflied shrimp sauteed in butter, garlic, and wine sauce with fresh mushrooms and parsley.

Pollo Primavera—boneless breast of chicken topped with a garden variety of fresh seasonal vegetables in a delicate cream and parmesan cheese sauce

Pasta Primavera—a beautiful combination of fresh seasonal vegetables in a tasty cream, butter and parmesan cheese sauce, combined with delicate linguini pasta

Pasta Primavera Salad

1/2 cup broccoli flowerets, lightly steamed
1 medium zucchini, sliced and lightly steamed
1 medium tomato, diced
1 cup mushrooms, sliced and lightly steamed
1/2 cup peas, cooked
2 tsp. dried basil
Pasta Primavera Dressing
1/4 lb. rainbow rotelli pasta

Cook pasta according to package directions until it is al dente. Rinse in colender and set aside.

Cool cooked vegetables. Mix them together, and add salt and pepper to taste. Add basil. Toss vegetables with pasta shells. Set aside.

Pasta Primavera Dressing:

2/3 cup white wine vinegar
1 3/4 tsp. Dijon mustard
1 1/3 cups vegetable oil
pinch of white pepper
1 1/2 tsp. fresh tarragon leaf, chopped

Mix together vinegar, pepper, and fresh tarragon. Add Dijon mustard, and blend well. Add vegetable oil and mix. Re-mix before each use.

Yields about 2 cups

Putting it all together:

Pour *Pasta Primavera Dressing* over vegetable and pasta mixture. Toss gently. Chill for two hours.
Garnish with orange slices, Romaine lettuce, or parsley.

Serves 4

Shrimp and Linguine Dijon

4 oz. butter
2 tbsp. fresh garlic, crushed
1 1/2 lbs. shrimp
1/2 cup Dijon mustard
2 eggs, well-beaten
3 cups cream
1 1/2 lbs. linguini noodles

Cook linguini according to package directions, adding 1 to 2 tbsp. oil to water. Drain and set aside.
Saute shrimp with garlic and butter. Add Dijon mustard, egg, and cream. Stir gently until blended, simmering just until heated through. Pour over cooked linguini. Garnish with parsley.

Serves 4

Pollo Cacciatore

4 boneless chicken breasts
4 oz. butter
16 oz. can tomato sauce
8 oz. marsala wine
1 lb. mushrooms, sliced
1/2 bell pepper, cut into strips
1 small white onion, sliced
3 stalks celery, sliced
1 handful black olives, sliced
2 cloves garlic, finely chopped
2 tbsp. olive oil

In skillet or saute pan, brown both sides of chicken breasts in butter. Reduce heat and continue to cook until chicken is half done. Remove chicken from skillet and keep warm.

In another skillet or saute pan, saute onions, garlic, bell pepper, black olives, and mushrooms in olive oil. Add tomato sauce and marsala wine and blend.

Add partially cooked chicken. Simmer until chicken is tender.

Serves 4

Palmier Bistro

902 W. Washington Street
San Diego, CA 92103
Phone: (619) 297-2993

This is a restaurant where the tastes of Southern California and the French Riviera come together. In a clean, bright setting of linen-covered tables on a checkered tile floor, Palmier Bistro offers a special blend of cuisine. There are light sauces and healthful cooking of "nouvelle cuisine" with ample servings of traditional French meals.

Sundays and Mondays, diners can try Owner-Chef Jean-Pierre's prix fixe French menu, which includes appetizer, choice of entree, and a delectable homemade dessert. Wednesdays and Thursdays, Chef Roberto from Rio de Janiero presents his own Brazilian specialties, a prix fixe menu that has become very popular among locals and transplanted Brazilians.

Palmier Bistro has a variety of alternatives for those who like fine food but aren't looking for a typical sit-down dining experience. Imported items from the well-stocked deli case can be packed up for a lunch or snack. But the restaurant also provides an ample carry-out menu, including prepared country picnics complete with eating utensils and napkins on request.

❖ *Hours: Brunch: Saturday, 9 a.m.-Noon; Sunday, 9 a.m.-2 p.m. Lunch: Monday through Friday, 11 a.m.-5 p.m.; Saturday, Noon-5 p.m. Dinner: Monday through Thursday, 5 p.m.-10 p.m.; Friday & Saturday, 5 p.m.-11 p.m.; Sunday, 5 p.m.-9 p.m.*

❖ *Casual attire; reservations recommended. Metered street and lot parking available. Price: Inexpensive to expensive.*

House Specialties

Crispy Sea Bass—a tender filet of fresh bass, wrapped in a thin potato slice, sauteed and served over a bed of snow peas with a xeres vinegar sauce

Poulet Forestiere—boneless chicken breast sauteed with mushrooms, fresh herbs, white wine, and shallots, in a delicate cream sauce

Pate, Fruit and Cheese Platter—generous assortment of pate, imported cheeses, and fresh fruits served with fresh French bread

Tarte Provencale

4 oz. whole grain mustard
Pate Brisee
3 medium tomatoes, sliced
Basil Garlic Cream Sauce
1/2 tsp. Herbes de Provence
1/2 tsp. fresh basil, chopped
1 1/2 tsp. garlic, chopped
1/4 cup swiss cheese
salt and pepper

Basil Garlic Cream Sauce:

1 1/2 cups milk
1 1/2 cups heavy cream
1 tbsp. butter
1 tbsp. flour

Pour milk and cream in pan with garlic and basil. Heat to boiling.

In a small pan over medium heat, make a roux by stirring butter into flour until thickened. (See "roux" in Glossary.)

Pour hot milk and cream mixture into the roux and cook over medium heat for three minutes. Set aside.

Pate Brisee:

1 cup flour
dash of salt
5 tbsp. unsalted butter, softened
1 egg yolk
4 tbsp. water

Preheat oven to 350 degrees.

Sift the flour and salt into a mixing bowl. Add butter and mix until a coarse texture is obtained. Make a well in the mixture. Stir the egg and water together, then add into the well in the flour mixture. Work mixture quickly to form a light dough. Roll out dough into 1/8" thickness.

Putting the Tarte Provencale Together:

Using a 10" oven-proof mold, put the dough inside the form. Add mustard, Garlic Basil Cream Sauce, tomato slices, Herbes de Provence, and swiss cheese.

Bake at 350 degrees for 30 to 35 minutes.

Serves 6-8

Pork Tenderloin Sandwich

1 1/2 lbs. pork tenderloin
6 oz. pine nuts, crushed to powder
6 oz. pistachio nuts, crushed to powder
3 oz. butter
2 eggs, whipped
all-purpose flour
3 to 4 tomatoes, sliced
1 red onion, sliced
small bunch fresh mint, chopped

Cut pork loin into thin slices. Dip each slice first in flour, then egg.

Dredge through mixture of pine and pistachio nuts.

Saute the pork in butter until golden brown (1 to 2 minutes on each side). Remove from pan. Cool and store in refrigerator.

To make sandwich, slice fresh baguettes into desired sandwich size. Slice each piece open. Layer each side with whole grain mustard. Add pork, sliced tomato, onion, and fresh mint.

Serves 6

Ratatouille Provencale

2 red bell peppers, seeded, cored, and sliced
2 green bell peppers, seeded, cored, and sliced
2 medium yellow squash, unpeeled and cubed
2 medium eggplant, unpeeled and cubed
2 medium zucchini, unpeeled and cubed
1 lb. diced tomato
2 medium brown onions, peeled and cubed
1 28-oz. can tomato puree
3 bay leaves
5 to 6 garlic cloves, chopped
1/2 cup virgin olive oil
2 tbsp. Herbes de Provence
1/2 cup water
salt and pepper to taste

In a large skillet, saute eggplant, zucchini and squash in half the oil until tender. In a separate pan, saute onions in remaining oil until golden brown. Then add peppers, tomatoes, herbs, salt, pepper, and tomato puree. Simmer until mixture thickens (about 15 minutes).

Add eggplant, zucchini, squash and water, and cook uncovered for 10 minutes. Season to taste. May be served hot or cold, as side dish or main course.

Serves 8

Poulet Forestier

12 to 16 half chicken breasts (2 per serving), boned and skinned
clarified butter (enough to brown chicken breasts)
1 1/5 lb. mushrooms, sliced
6 tbsp. fresh thyme, chopped
2 bunches fresh basil, chopped
1 1/2 cups heavy cream
3 tbsp. fresh garlic, chopped
juice from 2 lemons
dash of white wine

Lightly brown chicken breasts in clarified butter and garlic. Deglaze sautee pan by removing grease and adding white wine. Continue cooking while scraping the solidified juices from the sides of the pan.

Add mushrooms, thyme, and basil, and saute briefly. Add heavy cream and bring to a quick boil. Turn chicken breasts and allow sauce to thicken. Remove chicken breasts from pan and pour sauce lightly over top. Serve with rice and fresh steamed vegetables.

Serves 6 to 8

Scampi Provencale

8 oz. (about 10) jumbo shrimp, peeled, deveined, and butterflied
1 tbsp. fresh garlic, chopped
1 tbsp. shallots, chopped
1 tbsp. sun-dried tomatoes, chopped
2 tbsp. pine nuts
2 tbsp. butter
1 oz. sweet vermouth
2 oz. linguine pasta
2 oz. heavy cream
2 tbsp. fresh basil, chopped
2 tbsp. fresh tarragon, chopped
1 tbsp. fresh tomato, chopped

Cook linguine according to package directions.

In a saute pan, place butter, butterflied shrimp, herbs, and spices, and saute lightly. Deglaze pan by removing grease, and adding vermouth, continuing to cook while scraping solidified juices from sides of pan. Add cream. Cook until sauce thickens.

Remove shrimp from pan and serve over linguine. Pour sauce over shrimp.

Serves 2

Prince of Wales Grill

Hotel del Coronado
1500 Orange Avenue
Coronado, CA 92118
Phone: (619) 435-6611

Inside the Hotel del Coronado is the Prince of Wales Grill, named to commemorate the 1920 visit of the Prince of Wales who later abdicated the British throne to marry Wallis Simpson, a Coronado housewife. This is a dining room of old-fashioned elegance, with plush booths, flickering candlelight, and a feeling of exclusivity.

A prix fixe gourmet menu, including a full meal with dessert and coffee, is served nightly, but there is also a well-chosen selection of gourmet dishes on the regular menu. Balance, not volume, is the keynote of these selections. The menu is succinct, but variety has not been lost. The touch of a creative chef is apparent throughout.

Fish and shellfish are prepared in many different styles, as are meats and poultry. Even the menu descriptions are stimulating and inviting, and they offer the diner some tough choices. Appetizers, soups and salads are done with unusual sauces and dressings.

Class and quality are what the Prince of Wales Grill is all about, so naturally, the whole effort of kitchen and service staff is to make the guest feel like royalty.

❖ *Hours: Dinner: Tuesday through Sunday, 6 p.m.-10:30 p.m.*
❖ *Dressy attire; reservations required. **Fee parking** or valet parking available.*
Price: *Expensive. Major credit cards accepted.*

House Specialties

Veal Loin en Brioche—veal stuffed with lobster medallion, with a pickled shallot and red zinfandel glaze

Salmon Napoleon—thin layers of fresh salmon, sorrel, mushrooms, and tomatoes

Crown Rack of Lamb—roasted lamb with essence of merlot and mint

Pacific Bouillabaise

For the stock:

8 oz. clam juice
8 oz. white wine
2 tbsp. tomato paste
2 oz. olive oil
1 tbsp. fennel seed
1 carrot, peeled and chopped
2 stalks celery, cut into pieces
1 white onion, chopped
4 bay leaves
1 tsp. thyme
1 tsp. black peppercorns
1/2 tsp. cloves
12 threads saffron
2 tbsp. chopped garlic
shrimp shells (from 8 shrimp used in this recipe)
4 lemon halves
8 oz. water
salt and pepper to taste

Place all ingredients for stock into 2-quart pot and boil for 30 minutes. Strain and reserve.

For the Bouillabaise:

1 pint stock
8 whole clams
8 shrimp, peeled and deveined (Retain shells for use in stock.)
8 fish chunks (sea bass, snapper)
8 crab claws, washed
8 mussels, washed
8 scallops
leeks
turnips
carrots
tomatoes
seasoned sourdough croutons
fresh parsley, chopped

Cut leeks, turnips, and carrots into 2" matchsticks. Peel, seed, and dice tomatoes.

Put stock into a large saute pan and bring to a simmer. Add clams and mussels, and cook until they begin to open.

Add shrimp, scallops, and fish, and cook until just firm.

Add crab claws and vegetables and boil for 1 minute.

Divide among 4 bowls and sprinkle with chopped parsley.

Serves 8 if used as first course, 4 if used as entree

Chilled Apple Soup

5 to 6 green apples, peeled, cored, cut in eighths, and set aside in lemon water
2 oz. candied ginger (chopped)
juice of 4 to 5 limes
2 oz. Calvados apple brandy
1 pint apple juice
juice of 1 orange
1/3 bottle white wine (Riesling)
1/4 cup golden raisins
1 cup cream
1 cup plain yogurt
1 tbsp. fresh mint, chopped
1/8 tsp. each: cumin, allspice, and nutmeg (ground)

Remove apples from water and place in 4-quart stock pot with half the Riesling, half the Calvados, and all remaining ingredients, except the cream and yogurt.

Bring to a boil, and reduce to simmer. Cook for 20 to 30 minutes.

Remove from heat and force contents of pot through strainer. Puree ingredients that remain in strainer and return to the liquid.

Chill soup over ice. Whisk in yogurt and cream, and serve in iced glasses.

Serves 6-8

Ristorante Luigi Al Mare

Seaport Village
861 West Harbor Drive
San Diego, CA 92101
Phone: (619) 232-7581

Luigi's is a colorful Italian restaurant set on the boardwalk at Seaport Village, with an expansive view of the harbor, Coronado Bridge, and the Navy's aircraft carrier berth. (Usually, at least one of the huge carriers is visible.) Luigi's serves the freshest of seafood dishes, and patrons also will appreciate the fine pastas in light and tasty sauces. Salads are a delight of fresh ingredients. Appetizers are a tasty excuse to stop in and enjoy the view. The chef makes pastas from scratch and prepares veal in a variety of ways, including Veal Picatta, Veal Marsala, and an outstanding veal chop. His New York style cheesecake is a favorite among patrons.

Luigi's starts its Sunday brunch a little later than most restaurants, which means that if you're one of those folks who likes to sleep in, you won't miss any of the fun.

❖ **Hours:** *Brunch: Sunday, 11 a.m.-4:30 p.m. Lunch: Monday through Saturday, 11:30 a.m.-4:30 p.m. Dinner: Sunday through Thursday, 4:30 p.m.-10 p.m.; Friday & Saturday 4:30 p.m.-11 p.m.*

❖ *Casual attire; reservations recommended on weekends.* **Free parking** *for limited time in Seaport Village parking lots; parking rates apply afterward.* **Price:** *Moderate to expensive. Major credit cards accepted.*

House Specialties

Spit-Roasted Lemon Chicken
Fresh Pastas in a Variety of Sauces
Fruit of the Sea Platter

Bruschetta

(NOTE: This is a typical snack in Italy, which also can act as an appetizer.
It consists of thick-sliced, toasted bread with a tasty topping.)
12 ripe plum tomatoes, coarsely chopped
8 tbsp. shallots, chopped
6 tbsp. garlic, chopped
12 cloves garlic, slivered
2 cups fresh basil, chopped
7 tsp. lemon juice
1/2 cup extra virgin olive oil

Combine tomatoes with chopped garlic, shallots, basil, and lemon
juice in a bowl.

Saute slivered garlic in the olive oil until brown; discard garlic. Rub
olive oil on toasted bread. Top with tomato mixture.

Yields enough for about 12-15 slices of bread

Tri Colore

(NOTE: This dish is made with mozzarella de bufala, a soft ripening cheese that becomes creamier as it ages. Most mozzarella de bufala imported into this country is made with mild milk from both cows and water buffalo. Enjoy this with the reddest of sun-ripened tomatoes, fresh basil, and extra virgin olive oil.)

1 fresh tomato, sliced
1 ball mozzarella de bufala, sliced
fresh basil, cut into julienne strips
extra virgin olive oil
1 avocado (optional)

Lay tomato slices and cheese on chilled plate. Sprinkle with fresh basil and olive oil.

Garnish with a fan of avocado and a sprig of whole fresh basil.

Serves 4-6 as snack or appetizer

Salvatore's

750 Front Street
San Diego, CA 92101
Phone: (619) 544-1865

There is nothing about Salvatore's Cucina Italiana that will remind you of another Italian restaurant—unless you've been to Italy. Salvatore's sits like a jewel at the base of downtown's crown of condominium development, The Meridian. The restaurant's high ceilings, lovely tables, and Italian provincial decor done in ivory with rose accents, are a wonderful mix of Old and New World atmosphere.

Named year after year as the Gold Medal winner in the Italian food category of local restaurant competition, Salvatore's gives pasta a whole new meaning. There is nothing trendy about the pasta dishes here; you won't find fettucine and linguine languishing in lumpy cream sauces. Salvatore's serves a variety of unique pasta dishes, ranging from gently seasoned to very spicy.

The same subtle, but distinctive, taste is found in second courses. Raffaella Gangale, head chef and wife of the owner, Salvatore Gangale, makes a memorable presentation of beef, veal, chicken, lamb, fowl, and seafood.

❖ *Hours: Lunch: Monday through Friday, 11 a.m.-2:30 p.m. Dinner: Monday through Sunday, 5 p.m.-10 p.m.*
❖ *Dressy attire; reservations required. **Underground parking** validated after 5 p.m. Metered street parking available; free after 6 p.m. and on Sundays. **Price:** Moderate to expensive. Major credit cards accepted.*

House Specialties

Bavette al Granchio—linguine with hot, spicy crab meat sauce
Crespelle all 'Etrusca—crepes stuffed with assorted cheeses and
    mushrooms in tomato sauce
Cuscinetti di Vitella—scallops of veal folded with mozzarella and sauteed,
    with peas and mushrooms

Involtini di Melanzane

Rolled Eggplant

3 medium eggplants
1 can Italian tuna
8 fresh arrugula leaves
1 medium-sized lemon, cut into 1/8" slices
several tomatoes, each sliced into eight wedges

Peel eggplants. (Pick ones without many seeds. Usually, these are medium-sized and firm.)

Carefully slice eggplant to a thickness of 1/4", maintaining even slices. Sprinkle lightly with salt and let stand until drops of moisture form, approximately 5 minutes. Pat dry with towel.

Heat 2 or 3 sautee pans over medium heat with no oil in them. Place eggplant slices in pans, and cook until brown patches appear and slices have deflated by half. Set aside to cool.

Mix drained tuna with chopped capers and finely diced red pepper. Smear 1 or 2 tbsp. of tuna mixture on each slice of eggplant and roll up.

Assemble rolled eggplant slices on plate in a linear fashion, interspersed with tomato wedges.

Place 4 spears of arrugula on either side of the plate at an angle, and cover the stemmed ends with lemon slices.

Lightly coat eggplant and tomato wedges with **Vinaigrette**. Serve at room temperature.

Vinaigrette:

2 anchovies
3 tbsp. capers
2 tbsp. white wine vinegar
1/2 cup olive oil
1 small dried red chili pepper

Blend ingredients listed above in blender or food processor. The ratio of oil to vinegar must be to taste, depending on how anchovies affect flavor.

Serves 8-10

Tagliatelle al Papa Sisto
Fettuccine of the Pope

1/2 lb. Italian sausage, casing removed
1/4 white or yellow onion, chopped
1 pint heavy cream
1 tbsp. butter
1/4 cup parmesan cheese
1/4 cup grated mozzarella
salt and pepper to taste
1/2 lb. fettuccine noodles

In first sautee pan, brown sausage. Drain fat, and crumble.

In second sautee pan, saute onions in small amount of olive oil till clear. Drain.

Melt butter in a skillet. Add sausage and onion mixture. Sautee for 1 minute.

Add cream. Cook until reduced and thickened. Remove from heat. Add cheeses. Salt and pepper to taste.

Bring water to boil in stock pot. Add salt. Cook fettuccine noodles as directed on package.

Drain noodles and toss gently with sauce.

Serves 2 as entree, 4 as side dish

Penne all' Arrabiata

Angry Pasta

4 lbs. fresh Roma or plum tomatoes
1/4 cup olive oil
2 dried red chili peppers, crushed into small pieces
2 cloves fresh garlic, crushed
1 tbsp. fresh parsley, chopped and stems removed
parmesan cheese, grated
1 lb. penne pasta

Boil water. Blanch tomatoes for one minute. Peel, seed, and chop tomatoes.

Puree half of the tomatoes in blender. Chop the other half, set aside.

Saute garlic and chili peppers in olive oil until garlic begins to brown. Add the chopped tomatoes. Cook until partially done.

Add pureed tomatoes, letting sauce thicken and reduce.

Add parsley, salt, and pepper to taste.

Bring water to boil in stock pot. Add salt. Boil penne pasta as directed on package. Drain. Add sauce, mix, and add parmesan cheese.

Serves 4

Rigatoni alla Cornelia

1/2 cup fresh parmesan cheese, grated
3 fresh basil leaves, coarsely chopped
1/4 cup frozen peas, rinsed and drained
8 medium-sized mushrooms, cleaned and sliced
4 medium ripe tomatoes, blanched, skinned, and seeds removed
3 tbsp. olive oil
2 cups heavy whipping cream
1 lb. imported Italian rigatoni
1 clove garlic

Chop tomatoes. Saute 1 clove of garlic in olive oil until brown. Remove.

Add chopped tomatoes and simmer until soft. (If tomatoes used are acidic, add a pinch of sugar and/or bicarbonate of soda.)

Quickly puree tomatoes in blender, using on-off pulsing, leaving small chunks.

Saute sliced mushrooms in 2 tbsp. sizzling butter with a pinch of salt until just past firm.

Add 2 cups heavy whipping cream and reduce. When bubbles begin to form, add chopped basil, peas, tomato sauce, parmesan cheese, salt and pepper to taste.

Bring water to boil in a stock pot. Add salt. Cook rigatoni as directed on package. Toss gently in sauce. Garnish with chopped Italian parsley. Serve immediately.

Serves 4

Star of India

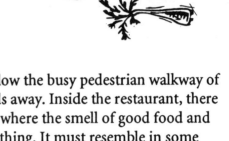

1025 Prospect Street
La Jolla, CA 92037
Phone: (619) 459-3355

Star of India is just a few steps below the busy pedestrian walkway of Prospect Street, but it seems like worlds away. Inside the restaurant, there is a peaceful, comfortable atmosphere where the smell of good food and the sound of soft Indian music are soothing. It must resemble in some small degree the experience of entering a residence in an Indian city where gardens and living quarters are sheltered from the tremendous bustle of humanity outside the doors.

Star of India offers a wide selection of dishes, both vegetarian and meat. Counting the snacks, rice dishes, vegetarian specialties, and hearty breads, there are no fewer than 20 non-meat items on the menu.

Star of India also offers a fine selection of tandoori specialties. The tandoori oven is a cylindrical clay oven heated by red-hot coals on the bottom, where temperatures can reach 800 degrees. To cook the breads, the chef must reach inside the oven to quickly press the raw dough against the oven walls. When it's done, he pries it loose with a kind of pick. Meats are barbecued on skewers that hang down into the oven. The high temperatures sear in the juices, leaving the meat succulent and tasty.

❖ *Hours: Brunch: Saturday & Sunday, 11:30 a.m.-3 p.m. Lunch: Monday through Friday, 11:30 a.m.-2:30 p.m. Dinner: Sunday through Thursday, 5 p.m.-10 p.m.; Friday & Saturday, 5 p.m.-10:30 p.m.*

❖ *Casual attire; reservations required.* **Metered street parking** *and fee parking available.* **Price:** *Moderate to expensive. Major credit cards accepted.*

House Specialties

Vegetable Pakora—various vegetables dipped in chickpea batter and fried

Tandoori Mixed Grill—assortment of marinated and spiced chicken, seasoned minced lamb, marinated cubed boneless lamb, and marinated prawns cooked in a tandoori oven

Navrattan Korma—vegetables, farmer cheese, and nuts in a mild cream sauce

Bengan Bhartha—eggplant baked in clay oven and cooked with onions, peas, and tomatoes

Prawn Bhuna—prawns in a spicy gravy of coconut and onions

Vegetable Biryani—saffron-flavored basmati rice with vegetables and nuts

Vegetables Pakora

Vegetables Fried in Chickpea Batter

1 large potato, sliced thin
1 medium-sized cauliflower, cut into flowerets
1/2 cup garbanzo bean flour
1/2 to 3/4 cup water
1 tsp. salt
1 tsp. cumin powder
pinch of cayenne pepper
pinch of asafoetida
1/2 tsp. turmeric powder
1 tsp. Garam masala (dried blended cardamom, cinnamon, bay leaves, cumin, coriander, and cloves)
vegetable oil for deep frying

In a bowl, combine flour and spices. Add water until it becomes like a medium-thick pancake batter.

Heat oil in wok until it is very hot. Dip cauliflower flowerets and potato slices in batter. Place into hot oil. (They will first sink to the bottom of the wok and then rise.)

Fry for 5 minutes and then stir occasionally until they are dark golden brown. Remove and drain on rack or paper towel. Serve with **Mint Chutney** and tamarind.

Mint Chutney:

1 bunch cilantro
1/2 bunch mint
3 green chilis
1/2 piece ginger
2 green onions
1 tsp. salt
1 lemon, cut in quarters
1 cup water or lemon juice
1/4 cup peanuts

Grind all ingredients to coarse texture in blender.

Serves 4

Aloo Gobi
Cauliflower and Potatoes With Herbs and Spices

2 cups cauliflower flowerets
2 potatoes, cut into 3/4" cubes
1 large brown onion, minced
1 small piece of ginger, cut fine
1/2 bunch cilantro, finely chopped
2 medium-sized tomatoes, chopped
2 green chilis, chopped
1 tsp. salt

1/2 tsp. cumin seeds
1/2 tsp. crushed coriander seeds
1/2 tsp. mustard seeds
1/2 tsp. red chili powder
1 tsp. turmeric
1 tsp. garam masala
4 tbsp. vegetable oil
butter

Rinse cauliflower and potatoes, and leave them in colander until ready to use.

In a sauce pan, use 1/2 stick butter to saute onions until slightly brown. Add ginger, garlic, chili powder, mustard seeds, cumin seeds, and coriander seeds, and let cook for 10 to 15 minutes.

Add chopped tomatoes, and continue cooking until mixture is a smooth paste.

Add cauliflower and potatoes to pan. Sprinkle a touch of water over the mixture, cover, and cook until vegetables are tender.

Remove from heat, and sprinkle with cilantro and Garam masala. Gently toss the mixture, and serve with rice or roti bread.

Serves 2

Navrattan Korma

1 lb. total mixed vegetables (potatoes, cauliflower, green peas,
    carrots, broccoli, and green beans)
1 quart whipping cream
1/2 tsp. turmeric powder
1/2 tsp. red chili powder
1/2 tsp. cumin powder
1 tbsp. coriander powder
1 green onion, chopped
1 tsp. garam masala
pinch of asafoetida
1 1/2 tsp. salt
butter for frying

Deep-fry all vegetables until cooked. Drain, and set aside.

In large sauce pan, put 4 tbsp. melted butter. Add turmeric, chili powder, cumin, coriander, and green onion. Fry for 30 seconds.

Add cream and garam masala, asafoetida, salt, and cooked vegetables. Cover for 15 minutes or until mixture thickens. Raisins and almond pieces may be added. Serve hot.

Serves 4

Basmati Rice

1 1/2 cups Basmati rice
2 tbsp. butter
1/2 tsp. salt
6 cloves
2 3/4 cups water

In a sauce pan, heat butter. Then add rice. Stir rice on medium heat for 1 minute.

Add water and spices, and bring to a boil. Cover and simmer for 15 minutes. Serve hot.

Serves 6

Chapatis (Roti)

2 cups whole wheat flour
2 tbsp. vegetable oil
1/2 to 3/4 cup water, as needed

In a bowl, combine flour and oil. Gradually add water until you have a soft dough.

Knead dough on floured table top. Divide dough into 12 pieces. Roll each piece into a ball, then press flat in the palm of your hand.

Place a cast iron skillet on medium heat, so it will be a bit hot when you are ready to cook the chapatis.

Roll flattened dough balls into 6" circles about 1/4" thick on a table or board covered with dry wheat flour. Try to make the chapatis as round as possible.

After rolling, place chapatis, one at a time, in the skillet. When the chapati starts to bubble on one side, turn it over, and cook on the other side. This takes about 20 seconds on each side.

Yields 12 chapatis

Dessert Kheer
Rice Pudding

6 cups milk
1 cup rice
1/8 cup golden raisins
1/4 tsp. cardamom powder
1/2 cup sugar
1/2 cup sliced almonds

In a large sauce pan, combine milk and rice. Cook on high heat for 15 minutes, stirring frequently. Bring to a rolling boil and reduce heat to simmer.

Continue cooking for 30 minutes or until ingredients thicken. Add sugar, raisins, almonds, and cardamon powder, mixing well.

Transfer mixture into dessert cups or a bowl. Refrigerate until cold. Serve cool.

Serves 4-6

Bengan Bhartha

1 large eggplant
1 large onion, chopped
1 large tomato, chopped
2 tsp. vegetable oil

1 tsp. salt
1/2 tsp. ground red chili pepper
1/8 tsp. garam masala
large pinch chopped cilantro

Over coals or open fire, char the eggplant until the skin becomes black and starts to split. Remove eggplant and cool. Peel off the skin and mash eggplant thoroughly in a bowl.

Saute onion in vegetable oil for about 5 minutes. Add tomatoes, salt, and red chili pepper, and saute 5 minutes more. Add eggplant and simmer for 10 minutes. Stir in garam masala. Garnish with cilantro.

Serves 4

Daal

1 cup lentils
3 cups water
1/2 tsp. salt
1/8 tsp. turmeric
1/4 tsp. ground red chili pepper
1 small onion, finely chopped
1 small tomato, finely chopped
1 tsp. vegetable oil
1/8 garam masala
large pinch cilantro, chopped

Boil together lentils, water, salt, turmeric, and red chili pepper. Reduce heat and cover the pan; simmer for about half an hour. Remove from heat when you can still see whole lentils, but they are well-mixed with water.

In a frying pan, saute onion in vegetable oil. When it becomes light brown, add tomatoes. When the tomatoes are cooked, add lentils and Garam masala. Blend. Garnish with cilantro.

Serves 2

Stefano's

3671 5th Avenue
San Diego, CA 92103
Phone: (619) 296-0975

To San Diegans, Stefano's is not just an excellent Italian restaurant. It's a committed member of the San Diego community. Taking an interest in charitable causes, presenting fascinating university extension classes, and staging superb celebrations of nearly every holiday, Stephen Zolezzi, owner, has made Stefano's an important part of the local scene.

The restaurant's "civic personality" is a bonus, however. The establishment rates with the best restaurants in town. Stefano's is substance, not just appearance. Guests can be assured of a wide array of fine Italian food, including homemade pastas in sauces of seafood, pesto, or other delectable ingredients. Pastas can be ordered in appetizer amounts or as main courses. Specialties with chicken, lamb, veal, beef, and Italian sausage are exquisitely prepared. Local fresh seafood is featured in a plentiful list of house specialties.

Stefano's has served visitors and locals for more than 25 years, winning many awards for its fine cuisine.

❖ **Hours:** *Lunch: Monday through Friday, 11 a.m.-2 p.m. Dinner: Monday through Thursday, 5 p.m.-9:30 p.m.; Friday & Saturday, 5 p.m.-11 p.m.; Sunday, 5 p.m.-8:30 p.m.*
❖ *Casual attire; reservations accepted.* **Metered street parking** *in daytime. After 6 p.m., free parking along streets and in nearby lots at Merkley-Mitchell Mortuary and Grossmont Bank.* **Price:** *Moderate to expensive. Major credit cards accepted.*

House Specialties

Linguine alla Pescatora—either shrimp, clams, or mussels, sauteed in olive oil, with broth, red pepper, and fine herbs, served over linguine pasta

Chicken Calafia—breast of chicken stuffed with Italian sausage, garlic, and Fontina cheese, in a sauce of pear tomatoes, basil, mushrooms, and cream

Agnella di Filetta—Loin of lamb stuffed with roasted garlic, marinated and grilled, with mustard sauce

Diavolo Fish Filet—Fresh fish filet sauteed with mushrooms and artichoke in a sauce of spicy wine, fresh tomato, and pepper.

Pollo Genovese

6 to 8 chicken breasts
1/4 cup olive oil
1/2 cup fresh mushrooms, sliced
1/8 lb. prosciutto, sliced and chopped
1/8 lb. gorgonzola cheese, cut into pieces
dash salt and pepper
1/2 cup fresh cream
1/2 to 3/4 lb. pasta (your favorite kind)

Cook pasta according to package directions. Set aside.

Cut chicken breasts into bite-sized pieces.

In a saute pan, heat olive oil. Add mushroom slices and chicken pieces.

When chicken is partially cooked, add prosciutto, gorgonzola cheese, cream, salt and pepper to taste. Reduce heat and cook until sauce has a creamy and light consistency. Pour over pasta, toss gently, and serve.

Serves 6-8

Pollo Calafia

6 chicken breasts, boned and pounded
1/2 lb. Italian sausage, skinned
1 tbsp. garlic, minced
4 oz. Fontina cheese, grated
4 oz. bread crumbs
2 oz. pesto sauce (Bottled pesto may be used.)
1/8 cup fresh parsley, chopped
1 tsp. thyme
1/4 cup olive oil
2 eggs

Preheat oven to 325 degrees.

Mix together Italian sausage, garlic, Fontina cheese, bread crumbs, pesto sauce, parsley, thyme, olive oil, and eggs. Fill chicken breast with mixture and roll closed.

Place chicken in baking dish with chicken stock. Cover and bake at 325 degrees for 30 minutes.

Calafia Sauce:

1/4 lb. butter
1 tbsp. garlic
8 oz. cream
1/2 lb. fresh mushrooms, sliced
4 pear or plum tomatoes, chopped
2 tbsp. pesto sauce
Parmesan cheese, grated

In saute pan, melt butter. Add all ingredients except Parmesan cheese. Heat until liquid is reduced.

Pour sauce over baked chicken breasts and top with Parmesan cheese.

Serves 6

Tango Grill

335 Market Street
San Diego, CA 92101
Phone: (619) 696-9171

A funny thing happens when guests begin to study the uncluttered menu at the small and lovely Tango Grill. The temptation arises to try more than one entree per person. You see a waiter delivering to a table of two a pan of Valencia-style paella, the yellow rice garnished with plentiful amounts of fish, shellfish, and crab legs. More than enough for two, you think. But 15 minutes later, the waiter is carrying to the same diners two plates of Lomo Buenos Aires, a tender, thick filet mignon wrapped in bacon, topped with a mushroom and sherry sauce, and accompanied by the famous Tango Grill provenzal potatoes. They won't be able to eat all that, you tell yourself. But the diners take their time, enjoying the soft Argentine music, friendly staff, and excellent food.

While every dish is quite ample, patrons do find it hard to settle on one entree at Tango Grill. That's because everything on the menu sounds so good. The chef prepares each meal individually. The beef is top quality; the steaks are incredible. Poultry and seafood are fresh. Sauces and seasonings are never overpowering, but always distinctive in flavor. Salads are freshly made, and dressing is delicious.

At Tango Grill, quality is consistent, and the menu concentrates on a very select variety of entrees. Some patrons drop by just for the homemade desserts, which include some Argentine adjustments to flan, cheesecake, and crepes. You might want to browse through the dessert descriptions, in fact, before trying two main dishes.

❖ **Hours:** *Dinner only, Tuesday through Sunday, 5:30 p.m.-10:30 p.m. Closed Mondays.*

❖ *Casual to dressy attire; reservations recommended.* **Metered street parking** *or fee parking available.* **Price:** *Moderate.*

House Specialties

Paella—saffron-seasoned rice and seafood dish with shellfish

Pollo en Escabeche—marinated chicken cooked and served cold with
    lemon slices

Argentine-style Beef—thick, large, juicy, and prepared with a sherry-
    mushroom or chimichurri sauce

Chimichurri Basting Sauce

2 cups fresh parsley, minced
1/2 cup fresh garlic, minced
1 1/2 cups olive oil
1 cup water
1/4 cup red wine vinegar
2 whole bay leaves
dash of paprika
dash of lemon juice
dash of ground red pepper (optional)

In a bowl, mix together bay leaves, paprika, and red pepper.

Heat 1 cup of water to a boil. Pour water over dry spices, and let stand until cool.

Add parsley, garlic, olive oil, vinegar, and lemon juice.

Refrigerate for 1 to 2 days. Use for basting fish, poultry or beef during roasting or grilling.

Yields about 3 cups

Argentine Salsa Criolla

(Note: This sauce may be used to season chicken, fish, or beef, or as a condiment.)

2 medium yellow onions
2 medium fresh ripe tomatoes, peeled and sliced 1/4" thick
2 medium sweet red pimento peppers, cut into strips
2 cloves fresh garlic, sliced very thin
1 tsp. fresh parsley, chopped
1 tsp. oregano
1 1/2 cups olive oil
1/4 cup red wine vinegar
dash of salt, pepper, and ground red pepper to taste

Boil whole onions until cooked, then chop coarsely.

Cut tomato slices into fourths. Mix together all chopped and sliced ingredients.

Add oregano, olive oil, vinegar, and red pepper, and salt to taste. Toss mixture thoroughly.

Sauce must be kept refrigerated. Just before using, add chopped parsley and black pepper.

Yields about 4 cups

Pollo en Escabeche

1 whole chicken
3 cups water
1 cup red wine vinegar
salt and pepper to taste
dash of paprika
2 lemons
2 to 3 tbsp. Giardiniere seasoning

Separate chicken into pieces.

In stock pot, cover chicken with water, and add red wine vinegar, giardiniere seasoning, and paprika. Cook at a low boil until tender.

Remove the chicken and reserve half the pan liquids. Place chicken in a bowl, and pour pan liquids over it as marinade. Let chicken cool slightly. Refrigerate chicken in marinade for 24 hours.

To serve, place cold chicken in serving dish with small amount of marinade to keep it moist. Squeeze juice of 1 fresh lemon on top. Cut second lemon into wedges and arrange on top of chicken for garnish.

Serves 4 as appetizer, serves 2 as entree

Thai House

3960 W. Point Loma Blvd.
San Diego, CA 92110
(619) 224-4871

No sooner had the intimate little Thai House Restaurant been opened than locals treated it as one of their favorites. Located in the Midway Towne Center shopping strip, this dining establishment brings to its guests the enticing, aromatic, sweet, spicy flavors of one of the most fascinating parts of the world.

Both Thai House chefs are natives of Thailand, but Chef Joy Elliott has resided in San Diego for years. Early on, she acquired local fame among friends and acquaintances for her superb culinary talents. It's reassuring to know that now, one can sample her exquisite work without having to wait for an invitation.

Thai House dishes are true to the mother country; their ingredients and preparation are authentic. Yet it is no trouble at all to simmer down the spiciness of certain hot dishes for the American palate. Diners also will be happy to know that MSG is not used here.

Patrons seem to favor almost everything on the menu, but curries, soups, noodle dishes and the incredible Thai herbal tea certainly top the list.

❖ *Hours: Monday-Saturday, 11 a.m.-9:30 p.m.; Sunday, 5 p.m.-9:30 p.m.*
❖ *Casual attire; reservations accepted.* **Parking** *in lot in front of restaurant.*
Price: *Inexpensive. Major credit cards accepted.*

House Specialties

Thai Iced Tea—herbal tea steeped in sweetened water, served over ice with half and half

Mussamun Chicken Curry—chicken cooked in a sauce of coconut milk, red chili paste, peanuts, kaffir lime leaves, curry, potatoes, and rice

Tom Kah Kai—spicy soup with a mixture of chicken, mushrooms, and herbs in coconut milk, served in a flaming Hot Pot

Thai House Beef—charbroiled tender beef, served with a dish of sauce made of lime juice, soy sauce, chilis and garlic, for dipping

Larb—a dish made of ground chicken or beef, seasoned with mint leaves, lime juice, onions, ground chili and rice powder.

Tom Kah Kai

Spicy Thai Chicken Coconut Soup

8 oz. boneless chicken, sliced into strips
4 or 5 thin slices galanga (Siamese ginger)
2 stalks fresh lemon grass, cut into 1" pieces
5 small green chilis, crushed
7 kaffir lime leaves, shredded
12 cilantro sprigs, shredded
1 to 2 green onions, finely chopped
2 cups coconut milk
2 cups chicken broth
1/4 cup fish sauce
1/4 cup lime juice

In a pot, bring chicken broth to a boil and add chicken, lemon grass, kaffir lime leaves, and sliced galanga. Bring to a boil.

Add coconut milk and boil for a few minutes until chicken is tender.

Add fish sauce and lime juice. Stir, and transfer to soup tureen.

Sprinkle with chopped green onions and cilantro leaves and serve.

Panang Gai
Panang Chicken

2 chicken thighs and 1 chicken breast, de-boned and cut
  into finger-sized pieces
1 cup coconut milk
1/4 cup vegetable oil
1/4 cup curry paste
1/4 cup peanuts, roasted and chopped
2 tbsp. palm sugar
2 tbsp. fish sauce
3 kaffir lime leaves, sliced very thinly

In a stir-fry pan or skillet, heat the oil over medium heat. Add the chicken and stir-fry until it is well-browned. Remove chicken and pour away most of the oil.

Add the curry paste to the remaining oil and cook over medium heat, stirring constantly.

Add coconut milk and bring to a boil. Continue to boil until liquid has reduced by half. Then add the peanuts, sugar, fish sauce, and chicken.

Stir well and cook until chicken is tender and has absorbed most of the liquid. Transfer to a serving plate and garnish with kaffir lime leaves.

Top o' the Cove

1216 Prospect Street
La Jolla, CA 92037
Phone: (619) 454-7779

It would be hard to think of a restaurant San Diegans like better than Top O' The Cove. It seems to have everything—setting, atmosphere, impeccable service, and truly outstanding food.

Situated along the restaurant row of Prospect Street, the historic building was constructed in 1884 as a beach cottage overlooking the spectacular La Jolla Cove and coastline. The interior, with its incomparable ocean view, is elegant and romantic. The patio leading into the restaurant is a perfect place to enjoy the soft breezes and colorful passersby. Two lovely settings, two different moods, in a restaurant that has been heralded by every major critic and fine food publication.

Top O' The Cove is noted for its entrees of duck, veal, roasted rack of lamb and filet of venison. The Sunday Brunch menu is extraordinary, with Eggs Sardou (eggs in a light sauce with artichokes), chicken crepes, and a seafood salad that comes with a considerable variety of fresh shellfish. Every dish—at brunch, lunch, or dinner—is prepared with a touch of class. Desserts are homemade by the restaurant's own pastry chef.

❖ *Hours: Brunch: Sunday, 10:30 a.m.-3 p.m. Lunch: Monday through Saturday, 11:30 a.m.-3 p.m. Dinner: Everyday, 5:30 p.m.-10:30 p.m.*
❖ *Casual attire in daytime, dressy at night; dinner reservations required.* **Metered street parking** *and fee parking available.* **Price:** *Expensive. Major credit cards accepted.*

House Specialties

Foie Gras de Canard—fresh sauteed duck liver nestled in a raspberry
  sauce
Cote de Veau Grille—grilled veal chop in a velvet sauce of cream and
  tarragon
Cote d'Agneau—roasted rack of lamb accented with the lightest curry
Medallions de Cerf—filet of venison with a sauce of fresh blueberries

Lobster in Champagne Sauce

3/4 bottle of Domaine Chandon Champagne
1 lb. lobster shells
4 1 1/2-lb. fresh lobsters
2 jumbo-sized carrots
2 medium brown onions, chopped
3 vine-ripened tomatoes, cut in quarters
1 stalk celery, chopped
1 large leek, chopped
6 fresh basil leaves, chopped
1 large bay leaf
fresh chervil, chopped
3 branches fresh thyme
juice from 8 oranges
8 asparagus per individual serving, steamed

Sauce:

In a stock pot, heat orange juice over low heat until it is reduced to a
glazy consistency. Add lobster shells, carrots, onions, thyme, bay leaves,
celery, leek, and tomatoes.

Cover ingredients with champagne. Cook on low heat, skimming top
occasionally.

When carrots are soft, remove large vegetables and lobster shells and
set aside.

Transfer pan liquids to a sauce pan, and reduce to a sauce consistency over medium heat. Turn off heat, and add chervil and basil.

Lobster:

Steam or poach lobster until done. Cut lobster through center and break claws.

Presentation:

Center asparagus on plate. Place lobster halves on sides of asparagus, moon-style with claws above halves. Surround lobster with sauce and reserved vegetables.

Serves 4

Venison in Fresh Fruit and Port Wine

7 oz. venison filet per individual serving
3 lbs. venison bones and trimmings
2 lbs. veal bones
3 medium onions, chopped
3 jumbo carrots, chopped
4 shallots, chopped
1 basket fresh mushrooms, cut in halves
36 snow peas, steamed
12 baby carrots
2 large bay leaves
2 branches fresh thyme
2 cloves garlic
4 pieces allspice
1/2 cinnamon stick
6 oz. fresh whole cranberries
6 oz. seedless grapes
3 oz. fresh blueberries or champagne grapes
1/2 cup ruby port wine

Sauce:

In a non-stick saute pan, saute onions and carrots for 5 minutes on low heat with no fat or butter.

Place carrots and onions in a large stock pot, along with venison bones, veal bones, half the blueberries (or champagne grapes), cranberries, bay leaves, thyme, allspice, cinnamon, garlic, and mushrooms. Cover with 12 quarts water, and cook on low heat for four hours, skimming occasionally.

Strain into a sauce pan. Reserve carrots. Continue to cook over low heat until liquid is reduced to light glaze consistency.

Add shallots and 1/4 cup port wine. Reduce to sauce consistency.

Add seedless grapes and the remainder of blueberries or champagne grapes.

Venison:

Grill venison filets on both sides for about 4 minutes.

Presentation:

Place venison filet at center of plate. Pour sauce around venison. Alternate three snow peas and baby carrots as border around filet.

Pheasant Breast with Shellfish in Champagne Sauce

4 half pheasant breasts	1/2 cup fresh baby corn
1/4 cup butter	8 jumbo shrimp, split in half
2 tbsp. flour	1 10-ounce lobster tail, sliced
1 cup champagne	8 ounces angel hair pasta
1 cup pheasant stock (or chicken stock)	4 ounces smoked ham
1 cup diced tomato	2 cloves garlic, chopped
1 cup baby peas	3 leaves fresh basil, chopped

Saute skinless, boneless pheasant breasts in butter. Add flour, champagne and pheasant stock, and cook until liquid reduces by half.

Add diced tomato, peas, and corn. Cook for two minutes. Then add shrimp, lobster, and angel hair pasta. Continue cooking for another two minutes.

Finally, add ham and remove from heat. Salt to taste and add garlic and basil.

Serves 4

Salade de Canard

Romaine lettuce, shredded
cantaloupe balls
fresh strawberries, sliced
Belgian endive
chives, chopped
Radicchio lettuce
juice from 1 orange

2 oz. balsamic vinegar
1 bay leaf
fresh thyme
2 oz. white wine (Chardonnay)
1 oz. vegetable oil
duck breast

Saute duck breast in a little oil until medium done. Remove from heat and let cool.

In small sauce pan, heat orange juice and balsamic vinegar. Reduce over low heat until liquid thickens.

Add bay leaf, fresh thyme, chardonnay, vegetable oil, and salt and pepper to taste. Reduce until thick.

Slice duck breast at 45-degree angle. Make mound of shredded romaine lettuce in middle of plate. Lay duck breast slices around mound. Garnish plate with cantaloupe, strawberries, endive chives, and radicchio lettuce. Pour warm sauce on top.

Serves 1

Lobster Bisque

1 1/4 to 1 1/2 lb. Maine lobster
1 carrot, peeled and cut into 1" pieces
1 yellow onion, peeled and cut into 1" slices
1 stalk celery, cut into 1" pieces
1 leek, cut into 1" pieces
1 bay leaf
fresh thyme
fresh tarragon
fresh basil
olive oil
1 1/2 tsp. cognac
1 tbsp. sherry
1 tbsp. white wine
1 oz. tomato paste
1/2 cup whipping cream
lemon juice

In stock pot, cook lobster in enough water to cover, plus 2 to 3 inches more. Cook slowly, about 15 minutes. Remove lobster, reserving broth.

Remove lobster meat from shells. Chop meat and set aside.

Cut shells into small pieces and cook in olive oil. When shells turn red, add cognac, sherry, and white wine. Cook for a few seconds longer.

Saute vegetables and spices in olive oil over low heat. To this pan, add lobster broth, shells, and tomato sauce. Add salt and pepper to taste.

Cook over low heat 30 to 45 minutes. Strain mixture through a fine sieve.

Combine strained mixture with cream. Add chopped lobster meat. In a sauce pan, cook cream and lobster over low heat until well-blended. Lemon juice may be added to taste.

Serves 4

Twelve Stars Cafe

412 University Avenue
San Diego, CA 92103
Phone: (619) 298-5200

Named in honor of the twelve countries that comprise the European Common Market, the Twelve Stars Cafe has a menu that highlights some of the best foods from these nations. An intimate, friendly place, the cafe is located in the village-like atmosphere of Hillcrest. San Diegans prize Twelve Stars Cafe for its individually prepared meals at excellent prices.

Owners Andre Vautrin and Danielle Renaud actually have made two dining establishments in one. Just inside the door is the cafe, where the menu is intriguing, but less complex. At the back of the room is the restaurant, with a full menu and linen-covered tables for dressier dining.

The menu does not contain Americanized versions of European dishes. It simply brings the vast array of California meats, seafoods, fruits, and vegetables into the creative hands of Vautrin, whose cuisine can be hearty and robust or light and delicate. There are many choices of soups, salads, and pastas, along with various meats, poultry, and seafood entrees.

❖ *Hours: Breakfast: Tuesday through Sunday in summer; otherwise, weekends only, starting 9:30 a.m. Lunch: Tuesday through Friday, 10:30 a.m.-2:30 p.m. Dinner: Tuesday through Sunday, 5:30 p.m.-10:30 p.m. Closed Mondays.*

❖ *Casual attire in cafe, casual to dressy attire in restaurant. No reservations required in cafe, but recommended in restaurant. **Parking** available at street meters, or use pay parking at Union Bank, corner of Sixth and University. **Price:** Extensive menu ranges from inexpensive to expensive. Major credit cards accepted.*

House Specialties

Paella—a traditional Spanish dish with rice, seafood, and
saffron seasoning

Entrecote Cafe de Paris—New York steak topped with herb butter
mousse

Bouillabaise—rich seafood soup with fresh fish, whole clams and
mussels, and shrimp, with a hint of saffron

Bouillabaise

1 quart fish stock
dash saffron
6 tsp. garlic, crushed
4 medium potatoes
16 whole mussels, washed
4 shrimp scampi, peeled and deveined
8 oz. halibut
8 whole clams, washed
8 oz. swordfish fillet (or any other fish with firm meat)
8 oz. monkfish

In a stock pot, boil fish stock. Add saffron and crushed garlic.
Boil and peel potatoes. Add potatoes to stock pot. Skim the stock.
Cut fish into large cubes. Add fish, along with mussels, shrimp, and
clams, to other ingredients. Cook briefly, just until boiling.
When serving, do not ladle soup from bottom of pot. Remove
seafood and potatoes with slotted spoon to avoid disturbing any sand or
shell fragments that might be present from mussels or clams.

Serves 4

Salmon Tartare

2 4-6 oz. salmon steaks (fresh, not frozen)
1 tsp. capers
1 tsp. parsley
1 tsp. chives
1 tsp. garlic
dash of fresh dill
1 small lemon
3 tbsp. olive oil
dash of salt and pepper

Cut salmon into 1" cubes. Cut stems off parsley.

In a food processor, add salmon, capers, parsley, chives, garlic, dill, lemon, olive oil, and salt and pepper. Grind ingredients on pulse setting, being careful not to puree. Serve on toast.

Serves 4

Beef Bourguignon

1 lb. top sirloin beef, cut into 2" cubes
dash of oregano
3 bay leaves
2 cloves garlic, crushed
3 carrots, peeled
half bottle of heavy, dark wine (burgundy, merlot, or cabernet)
1 tsp. beef bouillon
2 tsp. cornstarch
2 tbsp. sour cream

Marinate cubed beef, peeled carrots, crushed garlic, oregano, bay leaves in red wine for 24 hours.

The next day, drain meat. Reserve wine for use in cooking the stew.

In a skillet, sizzle beef cubes until they have a light brown color. With a slotted spoon, remove meat from fry pan and put into a stew pot.

Dissolve bouillon in 1 cup water and add to pot. Add the reserved wine marinade until meat is covered.

Cook over low heat until meat is tender. To thicken stew, sprinkle with cornstarch. Taste for seasoning. Stir in sour cream.

Can be served with country potatoes, rice, or pasta.

Serves 4

Seafood Salad

Salad:

mixed lettuce (iceberg, butter, red leaf, etc.), washed and torn   into small pieces
1 small bunch radishes, sliced or quartered
1 cucumber, peeled and sliced
2 tomatoes, sliced
1 carrot, grated
1 stalk celery, minced
2 tsp. garlic, chopped
dash of fresh parsley, fresh tarragon, and fresh chives

Artistically arrange lettuce, tomatoes, cucumber, and radish on plate. Sprinkle with grated carrot, minced celery. This arrangement becomes salad bed for seafood.

Seafood:

4 large fresh scallops
4 large fresh clams
8 fresh mussels
8 oz. mixed fish (halibut, salmon, rock fish, bass, red snapper),
    cut into 1" cubes

(NOTE: Clams and mussels may be steamed and lifted carefully from pot with slotted spoon.)

Vinaigrette Dressing:

1 tbsp. spicy Dijon mustard
1 tbsp. red wine vinegar
3 tbsp. olive oil
salt and pepper

Mix above ingredients thoroughly.

Putting it all together:

In non-stick saute pan, use 2 tbsp. oil. Heat until very warm. Add seafood, including steamed mussels and clams, seasoning, salt and pepper. Mix carefully until seafood color is blond. Add garlic, parsley, tarragon, and chives.

Set mixture on bed of lettuce and pour vinaigrette over top.

Serves 4

Escargots a la Tequila

2 tbsp. oil
1/4 cup chopped onion
1 clove minced garlic
32 small escargots
1 cup brown sauce (or canned beef gravy)
1 cup half-and-half
1/2 cup small diced cactus (nopales), optional
2 tbsp. chopped green pepper
4 rounded tsp. paprika
1/2 tsp. ground pepper
1 cup fresh diced tomatoes
1/2 cup chopped green onions
1 tbsp. tequila

Over high flame, heat oil in heavy pan. Quickly saute onion until it begins to brown just slightly. Add garlic and saute about 10 seconds.

Add escargots; saute about 2 minutes. Add brown sauce, half-and-half, cactus, green pepper, paprika, and ground pepper.

Cook rapidly, about 3 minutes, stirring frequently, to reduce and thicken sauce. Add tomatoes and green onions. Heat through, about 1 minute.

Stir in tequila. Serve immediately. As appetizers, mixture may be served in ramekins; as entree, it may be poured over rice.

Serves 6 as appetizer, serves 4 as entree

Chocolate and Cointreau Mousse

1 orange
8 oz. semi-sweet chocolate squares
1 cup heavy cream
1 tbsp. Cointreau or Triple Sec

In a small pan, place chocolate, zest of orange, and juice of orange. Melt over moderate heat in Bain Marie (or double boiler). Add Cointreau. Mix gently. Refrigerate.

Whip the cream in chilled bowl until stiff peaks form. Add the chocolate mixture to the cream and turn delicately with spatula until smooth. Put into ramekins or glass bowl and cover with plastic wrap.

Refrigerate at least 2 hours.

Serves 4

Yakitori II

3740 Sports Arena Blvd.
San Diego, CA 92110
Phone: (619) 223-2641

Yakitori II has become one of the most popular Japanese restaurants in San Diego, and that is principally because its menu caters both to mainstream tastes and to those who really enjoy the authentic tastes of Japanese specialties. Patrons not fond of sushi rolls or sashimi are not overlooked. Chicken and beef yakitori—-marinated, skewered, and grilled—are favorites, as well as the stir-fry dishes and vegetables fried in a light, crispy tempura batter.

Both sashimi and a variety of sushi rolls may be ordered from the regular menu, but those who want a more expanded selection of these beautifully prepared specialties may indulge at the sushi/yakitori bar alongside the dining room.

Sushi is the term generally applied either to sliced fish on a bed of seasoned rice or rolls made of raw fish or vegetables surrounded by rice and wrapped in dried seaweed. Yakitori is a variety of barbecued foods, prepared and served immediately.

❖ *Hours: Lunch: Monday through Friday, 11 a.m.-2:30 p.m.; Saturday &*
Sunday, Noon-3p.m. Dinner: Everyday, 5 p.m.-10 p.m.
❖ *Casual attire; reservations recommended. **Free parking** in lot in front of*
*restaurant. **Price:** Inexpensive to moderate. Major credit cards accepted.*

House Specialties

Yakitori and Kushiyaki—skewers of tender chicken and beef grilled over an open fire with special sauce.

Tempura—large shrimp and fresh vegetables deep-fried in delicate, crispy tempura batter

Sukiyaki—tender beef sauteed in sukiyaki sauce with tofu, scallions, shiitake mushrooms, yam noodles, and nappa cabbage

Sushi—a variety of raw fish or vegetables sliced on a bed of seasoned rice or rolled with dried seaweed

Sukiyaki

1 1/2 lb. ribeye steak, thinly sliced
1/2 bunch green onions, cut into 2" pieces diagonally
1 bunch spinach, roots removed and chopped into 4 parts
4 to 8 pieces shiitake mushrooms
1 package roasted tofu (Yaki-dofu), cut into 1" cubes
1 package Shirataki noodles, drained and cut into 2" lengths
2 oz. beef fat

Sukiyaki Sauce:

1/2 cup soy sauce
1/2 cup Mirin (Japanese cooking wine)
1/2 cup water
3 tbsp. sugar
1 tbsp. Dashinomoto (fish powder that is added to water to make stock, it can be found in Oriental food stores.)

Arrange beef and vegetables on large platter. Boil 1/2 cup soy sauce with other ingredients for sukiyaki sauce and set aside.

Preheat large skillet on the table. (Sukiyaki is traditionally prepared at the table.) Add pieces of beef fat in the skillet, and rub on bottom to grease.

Place 1/3 of the beef in the skillet, and pour just enough sukiyaki sauce over the beef to cover. Turn beef over a few times, and add portions of vegetables and other ingredients. Keep them in separate groups in skillet.

Serve and eat while cooking. Add more ingredients and sukiyaki sauce to replenish skillet as needed.

Serves 4

Yet Wah

Glasshouse Square
3146 Sports Arena Blvd., Suite 37
San Diego, CA 92110
Phone: (619) 223-9800

Yet Wah is a quiet, tastefully done hideaway specializing in Mandarin Chinese cuisine. The vast relief covering most of one wall depicts the busy comings and goings of an ancient Chinese city. The combination of rich wood, gilt-edged ceiling tiles, red tablecloths and rattan-backed chairs provide a feast for the eye.

Yet Wah's menu is a feast for the palate. There are ample selections of vegetarian, beef, chicken, duck, and seafood entrees, all served with perfectly steamed rice. Appetizers include old favorites like Pot Stickers and Foil-Wrapped Chicken, along with the tasty Po Po Platter, served with a tiny grill on which guests can cook their own skewers of thin-sliced marinated meat.

Yet Wah in San Diego is the sister of the venerable Yet Wah in San Francisco, which has operated successfully for many years. The restaurant here is becoming an old standby as well, for the number of regular customers grows each year.

❖ *Hours: Lunch: Monday through Saturday, 11 a.m.-3 p.m.; Sunday, Noon-3 p.m. Dinner: Sunday through Thursday, 3 p.m.-10 p.m.; Friday & Saturday, 3 p.m.-10:30 p.m.*

❖ *Casual attire; reservations accepted.* **Parking** *in shopping center lot or on side streets.* **Price:** *Inexpensive. Major credit cards accepted.*

House Specialties

Yet Wah's Lettuce Blossom—pork, vegetables, and seasonings, stir-fried
and wrapped in lettuce leaves

Szechuan Spicy Lamb—spicy, hot dish of sliced lamb cooked with hot
pepper and fresh vegetables

Jewel Chicken—diced fried chicken topped with lychee fruits, mandarin
oranges, cherries, dragon eyes fruits, pineapples, and peaches

See Woo Duck—chunks of duck meat cooked with barbecued pork,
abalone, snow peas, and mushrooms in sauce

Lettuce Blossom

(Note: Dice or chop all ingredients, as specified, before proceeding.)
Heat wok. Then add 2 tbsp. salad oil.
Stir-fry in order:

1/2 tsp. garlic, chopped

1/2 lb. pork butt, minced
Season pork with:

3/4 tsp. salt

1 tsp. sugar

1 tbsp. soy sauce
Then add:

1/4 cup waterchestnuts, diced

1/4 cup bamboo shoots, diced

1/4 cup celery, diced

1/4 cup carrots, diced

1/4 cup brown onion, diced

2 Chinese dry black mushrooms, soaked in water, drained, and chopped

handful of green peas

Stir-fry all ingredients over high heat. Then sizzle 1 1/2 tsp. Chinese
cooking wine down side of wok.

Then add:

1/2 tsp. sesame oil

2 tbsp. peanuts, finely chopped

pepper to taste

Mix ingredients together. Wrap in lettuce leaves. Serve.

Serves 2-3

Foil-Wrapped Chicken

8 6"-square sheets of aluminum foil

1/2 lb. chicken meat, cut into 24 thin slices

Put chicken in bowl.

Then add:

1/2 tsp. Chinese cooking wine

1 1/2 tsp. soy sauce

1/2 tsp. Hoisin sauce

1/2 tsp. oyster sauce

1/2 tsp. plum sauce

1/2 tsp. ketchup

1/4 tsp. salt

1/4 tsp. sesame oil

1 tbsp. green onion, chopped

Mix chicken meat with all ingredients. Place 3 slices of chicken on each sheet of aluminum foil. Wrap to form sealed triangular packets.

Heat oil in wok. Deep fry the foil-wrapped chicken over high heat for about 5 minutes. Remove and drain. Then place on serving plate.

Serves 4 as appetizer

Glossary

Armagnac—brandy from the Gascony region of France

arugula—a type of green, like chicory, strong-tasting but not bitter

asafoetida—an extract of plant resin, dried and crushed, with a strong, distinct flavor; sold in powder form and used in some Indian and Middle Eastern dishes

Balikat jap—Indonesian soy sauce, available at specialty stores

bamboo shoots—the young, tender shoots of the tropical bamboo plant which are used as a vegetable

Basmati rice—fine, long-grained Indian rice grown at the foot of the Himalayas

black mushrooms—a type of mushroom used often in oriental dishes, commonly sold dry in sealed packets and requiring reconstition in water

black truffles—irregularly shaped black fungi that grow beneath the soil and are prized for their rarity and distinctive flavor

blanch—to scald an ingredient in boiling water in order to remove the skin or to lighten the color

bouquet garni—a mixture of herbs tied together or enclosed in a container or cheesecloth, used to season during cooking, and removed before serving

butterfly—to cut and spread open and flat

chilis—any of several varieties of hot peppers, the spiciness of which varies with the type. Common varieties include: yellow, California, serrano, jalapeno, and Anaheim.

candied ginger—ginger crystallized with sugar, one of the most common preparations of ginger

capon—a young, large male chicken, castrated, fattened, with exceptionally tender meat

carmelized sugar—sugar that is melted over low heat

cassoulet—a traditional dish from the Languedoc region of France, using beans, pork rinds, meat garni and gratin topping

chervil—aromatic herb the leaves of which are used in cooking

chilis—any of several varieties of hot peppers, the spiciness of which varies with the type. Common varieties include: yellow, California, serrano, jalapeno, and Anaheim.

chimichurri sauce—a tasty, seasoned Argentine sauce used to baste barbecued meats

chutney—a sweet-sour condiment made of fruits or vegetables (or a combination of the two) cooked in vinegar with sugar and spices (almost like a jam)

cilantro—the parsley-like leaves of coriander, known for a delightfully pungent flavor

clarified butter—butter from which the sediments have been removed; this is accomplished by melting butter over low heat, then letting it stand a few minutes, so that solids can settle to bottom and pure liquid can be skimmed from top

cornichons—a variety of small cucumbers bathed in brine and pickled in vinegar

corn milk—the liquid extracted from corn kernels

corn pulp—combination of corn kernels removed from the cob and combined with corn milk

creme fraiche—thickened, cultured cream with a sharp, but not sour, flavor; French dairy specialty; can be purchased in some grocery or specialty stores

creuset pot—a heavy pot made of enamel over cast iron

croutes—small slices or shaped pieces of bread (preferably French bread) prepared in a variety of ways: toasted; lightly browned in butter; fried in oil, or dried in the oven

dashinimoto—fish powder added to water to make stock; can be purchased in oriental food stores

deglaze—a method of coloring and flavoring stock by draining fat from pan in which meats have been sauteed, adding wine or stock, and cooking until carmelized meat juices have dissolved completely

dredge—to coat with flour or other dry ingredient

fennel—the anise-flavored plant commonly known for its aromatic seeds; however, the leaves, stalks, and root (or head) may be used in various dishes

flame or flambé—to drench with a liquor and ignite

foie gras—raw, semi-cooked, or preserved goose liver specially prepared before use; a traditional French specialty; can be purchased in gourmet section of grocery store or in specialty store

fontina cheese—Italian cow's milk cheese with brushed crust, nutty flavor

galanga—Siamese (Thai) ginger; available in oriental specialty stores

giardiniere seasoning—commonly purchased as a pre-mixed medley of Italian seasonings and herbs; usually available in gourmet section of grocery store or in specialty store

garam masala—a combination of such sweet spices as cardamon, cinnamon, nutmeg, coriander and cloves, as well as black peppercorns; available from Indian or Middle Eastern specialty markets

garbanzo bean flour—flour made from the broad, flat garbanzo bean, rich in Vitamins B and E and proteins; available from Indian or Middle Eastern specialty markets

garlic in oil—olive oil into which garlic cloves have been placed for flavor; may be made at home or purchased, and stored in glass bottle

golden raisins—light-colored raisins made from green grapes

gorgonzola—Italian cow's milk cheese, yellow with blue streaks; may be purchased in mild or strong varieties; available in grocery deli sections or Italian specialty markets

guacamole—mashed, seasoned avocados

Herbes de Provence—mix of dried aromatic herbs, including rosemary, thyme, basil, bay leaves, and summer savory; traditional French seasoning; available in gourmet section of grocery stores or in specialty markets

Hoisin sauce—spicy, thick, dark, sweet oriental sauce

hummous—cooked chickpeas crushed and mixed with sesame oil, used in Arab and Greek cuisine

Italian tuna—tuna packed in olive oil; available in Italian specialty markets

kaffir lime leaves—small, aromatic leaf from the kaffir lime plant, available only in oriental specialty stores

Kitchen Bouquet—a brand name liquid added to soups and other cooking liquids for color and flavor

leek—an onion-like plant the base (white part) of which is used to season soups and other dishes or is cooked by itself as a vegetable

lingonberries—a mountain berry grown primarily in Scandinavia; available in gourmet or specialty section of grocery or in specialty markets

mango—a deliciously sweet, almost tangy fruit with a flat oval shape and a long seed; grown in tropical climates

Marsala wine—full-bodied wine from the Sicilian town of Marsala

mascarpone—Italian cream cheese; available in Italian specialty markets

matzo meal—crumbs made from unleavened crackers known as matzos

Mirin—Japanese cooking wine

monkfish—ocean fish with scaleless body and lean flesh that has a texture and flavor similar to lobster

mussels—bivalve mollusks with dark shells; they must be scrubbed before use, and any mussels that do not close when tapped should be discarded

nappee—a French cooking term describing a texture of sauce that permits coating and adhesion

ossobucco—a traditional dish of Milan, a type of stew made with veal shank

pate—a molded paste made of a variety of seasoned ingredients; a dough or a batter

pate brisee—light dough for a pastry shell

penne pasta—pasta shaped into tubes, cut at an angle, with ridged surface

pine nuts—small seeds from the cones of certain pine trees

porcini mushrooms—distinctively flavored mushrooms harvested in Italy during fall and early spring; available in gourmet sections of grocery stores or in Italian specialty markets

prix fixe menu—a fixed-price menu usually including soup or salad, entree, bread, beverage, and sometimes dessert

prosciutto—spicy Italian ham

quiche pan—ceramic, oven-proof pie pan with fluted sides

ragout—well-seasoned meat/vegetables cooked to a thick consistency like a stew

radicchio—red-leafed chicory that looks like a small curly red cabbage

ramekins—small, round, straight-sided souffle dishes; custard cups

rigatoni—short, wide-tubed pasta with ridged surface

risotto—short-grained rice grown in Northern Italy; often prepared by frying until brown, then cooking in stock

root celery—variety of celery grown for its root rather than its stalk

roux—thickening base made of flour slowly heated in a dry heavy pan, then cooked in an equal amount of butter; roux can be cooked little if used as base of white sauce, and longer (in order to brown it) if used as base of brown sauce

saffron—the dried orange stigmas of the crocus flower sold as thread or yellow powder; turmeric may be used as a substitute for this very expensive, unique seasoning

scald—to bring almost to a boil

shallots—an onion-type plant with a milder flavor; its bulb is used in cooking

shiitake mushrooms—a mushroom used in oriental cooking, usually sold dry in oriental food stores or grocery sections

shiretaki noodles—clear yam noodles sold in the can or fresh in a sealed tub

sieve—to force ingredients through mesh material or strainer to make fine particles

springform pan—a baking pan with removable sides

sieve—to sift or strain ingredients

sun-dried tomatoes—tomatoes dried in the sun and packed in oil

sweat—to heat just until moisture beads appear on surface

tabouleh—an Arabic salad of marinated bulghur wheat, tomatoes, and seasonings

tagliatelle—folded egg or spinach noodles, thinner than fettucini

tarragon vinegar—sprigs of tarragon blanched and marinated in white wine vinegar

terrine—deep ceramic, ovenproof dish with straight sides, handles, and tight-fitting lid

toast points—a small, triangular-cut, toasted piece of bread

tofu—soybeans pureed and congealed, with a soft, cheese-like texture

tomatillo—small, tart, green tomatoes covered with dry brown skin

tortellini—small, meat- or cheese-filled pasta

tortelloni—meat-filled pasta slightly larger than tortellini

truss—to tie legs and wings into place on chicken, turkey, or fowl

tureen—a wide, deep bowl with handles, lid, and usually a slot for a ladle; used for serving soup

water chestnuts—the tuber of an aquatic plant usually sold canned and sliced; crunchy consistency and lightly sweet taste

whey—the watery part of milk or other foods that remains after coagulation or cooking; the semi-liquid coating on meat that remains after cooking

xeres—unique sherry vinegar

yam noodles—dried noodles made from yam flour

zest—colored portion of citrus skin, grated

Index